WHEN THE LIGHT GOES OUT

A Psychiatrist's Journey of Trauma, Grief and Change

A Guide to Understanding and Normalising
Mental Health and the Tools for Overcoming
Adversity in Everyday Life

DR LISA MYERS

I know the pain of past trauma and anxiety all too well. The 'trauma snowball effect' Lisa speaks of, can truly affect your quality of life. However, when trauma is well managed, it allows one to live a meaningful and peaceful existence. Something everyone deserves.

Lisa's book and work is just so important. I hope anyone struggling in silence has access to these life changing tools Lisa speaks of. Anxiety and trauma must be managed holistically, and when it is – you really can heal. Medication, therapy, wellness – can all be incredibly transformational.

Let be and embrace. Something this book can teach so many of us.

Jessica Sepel – Founder of *JSHealth*

Dr Lisa Myers' authentic writing style makes this deep, troubling, and complex work a compelling read. Her brutal honesty allows one to share the raw pain, and loss of centre, experienced by a victim of trauma.

As a well-respected psychiatrist, she has the courage to tell her story and admit to her symptoms and this certainly de-stigmatises mental health issues. Her story also provides a service to victims of trauma who hopefully will receive more understanding and support because of her explicit sharing.

I thank Lisa for changing the narrative where mental health professionals are judged negatively when our lives are not perfect. Lisa provides a more viable and truer picture where no-one is immune. She role-models that a clinician who is committed to her patients, and seeks therapeutic assistance herself, can share their journey with deeper empathy and insight.

Renee Mill – Clinical Psychologist and bestselling author of *Anxiety Free, Drug Free*

Gosh, at times I could barely breathe, at times I chuckled out loud and I cried and cried. Amazing, Lisa, congratulations on a beautiful piece of work!

Dr Wendy Duncan – Child and Adolescent Psychiatrist

A heart-centred book on trauma, vulnerability and hope. Lisa's authenticity reminds us that we are all imperfect, yet beautiful; and capable of finding light when all feels lost.

Pamela Espin – AMHSW

I could not put it down. Lisa's book will resonate with so many trauma survivors.

Anonymous – Trauma Survivor

Lisa's sincere and vulnerable story is unapologetically honest and beautiful. Just beautiful! Such an interesting read. Bravo!

I connected with her approach to 'just doing, disconnect and keep going – to Just Do.' As all working mums know, this is sometimes how we get by. Is it the answer? No.

Self-compassion and nurturing are how we truly survive and thrive and Lisa's book is a testament to this.

'To grow, like to grieve is a boundless process' …. 'Life is the lesson' - beautiful. Lisa, thank you for sharing your story. This is an amazing book!

D'Leanne Lewis – Principal Laing+Simmons Double Bay and Director Laing+Simmons National Corporation, Star *Luxe Listings Sydney*

Lisa's openness, honesty and humanness is all there in spades. It made me cry more than once and certainly took me on my own journey. I slowed down and thought more about aspects of my own life. I absolutely loved the way that the clients' stories were woven through it.

Dr Sarah Marshall – Psychologist

A captivating, compelling and beautifully written book, skillfully merging personal and expert insight into trauma and grief. Dr Lisa Myers guides readers through her own experiences, willingly sharing her own vulnerability and struggles, in doing so, creating a wonderful book.

Tamar D. Black, PhD – Educational and Developmental Psychologist and Author, *ACT for Treating Children.*

Dr Myers has written an insightful account of trauma, skilfully linking her deeply personal and moving account with her years of experience as a psychiatrist in this field. Highly recommended for both clinicians and individuals affected by trauma.

Dr John Lam-Po-Tang – Consulting Psychiatrist

For Dad.

Thank you for giving me this story to write.

Contents

PART 1

My Story

Life always gives us a chance to grow
even if we don't like the lessons.

Prologue

I was greeted by a friendly salesman in the Vodafone store. I needed a new screen protector for my phone, and he kindly found me the right one.

'Would you mind helping me to fit it? I'm not very good at these things,' I asked. As he opened the packaging and removed the cover, I admired his craftiness. *Why do I find these small tasks so tricky?*

'Thank you,' I smiled as I casually thought about the rest of my afternoon and the upcoming appointments with clients in my psychiatry practice.

Out of the corner of my eye, I caught a glimpse of a cylindrical stationery holder positioned on the far side of the desk.

In it was a red box cutter. Just an everyday tool used by ordinary people to open boxes, with a protruding triangular blade to rip through cardboard. It appeared macroscopic; although, it was probably just a regular-sized one.

Suddenly, my peripheral vision blurred. My heart rate shot up. All I could focus on was the bright-red object and the smooth, glistening, razor-like blade. My body remained in the Vodafone shop as my mind spun off far away. I saw the shop attendant mouthing his reply, but I couldn't hear his words. My wild heartbeat felt audible in the quiet of the shop.

In that moment, I wanted to run from the store, but couldn't without looking insane.

I took a deep breath as words filled my mouth behind my pursed lips. I swallowed hard so as not to blurt them out.

I thanked him and left the shop in a hurry, my heart racing as horrific memories circled in my head.

This is how trauma lives in us: the simplest tasks of my ordinary life have been forever invaded by an everyday object that can never be benign again.

As a psychiatrist, I know all too well how past trauma remains forever part of a person's life. Every trauma victim has their 'box cutter' – an object, sound, colour, image or situation that unexpectedly reactivates an intrusive thought or memory, casting a dark filter over the present moment. These evoke immense anxiety and the compulsion to act. For many years, I've been the one to hold the space for others, reassuring them that as they slowly recover from trauma, the constant reminders will lose their shocking power and become like a video playing in their minds – they will never stop replaying it, but it will fade in intensity and become background noise with which they do not need to engage.

But I am also just an ordinary person – and this is the story of my own trauma which has taken me on a journey to greater understanding, growth and self-acceptance. I hope, by sharing it here with you, to normalise, demystify and humanise the narratives around mental heath.

A Warning and Invitation to My Reader

I would give anything in the world to not have to include this warning, but sadly, my story requires it.

People turn to me as an expert in mental health for answers in the midst of their uncertainty. I always do my best to offer all my knowledge, skills and experience, just as I'm about to share my trauma and strategies for managing my grief with you in this book.

But in the pages that follow, you will come across references and scenes that are emotionally difficult and graphic; and for this reason, they could be triggering and traumatising.

If references to suicide, violence and abuse are topics that you know or suspect could cause you distress, I encourage you to seek guidance and support from a trained professional before reading this book. If you choose to continue and experience upsetting thoughts, feelings or urges, please stop and look after yourself. If necessary, contact your local services for support.

I am sharing my story to heal, not harm. Please help

me to make sure I do this.

I also need to confess my own vulnerability while I was working on this book. I've been intermittently anxious about how the personal nature of what I've divulged might be scrutinised and judged by my colleagues. Some might view my openness as unprofessional and my opinions, biased or limited. I've been concerned that I will be criticised for not having sufficiently covered the topic of trauma in all its manifestations and nuances. It has never been my intention to provide a comprehensive text on the treatment of trauma, but simply to share my experience both personally and professionally. Despite these fears, I have prepared myself for whatever judgements are forthcoming and welcome useful feedback. I've done my utmost to share my story here in the way I believe will be most helpful to readers.

I have changed the names of clients and most family members to protect their identities and honour their privacy. But with their consent and permission, I have kept the real names of my siblings and children who regard this book as part of their father and grandfather's legacy.

I do not, for a moment, wish to glamorise the challenges of working in the field of mental health. It is incredibly hard work and filled with many difficult moments and often relatively, minimal success.

All I am offering in the pages that follow are my own authentic experiences as a daughter, mother and psychiatrist. My hope is that my story provides you with support, comfort and guidance as you navigate your own path, when you find yourself in a time in your life when the light has gone out.

CHAPTER 1

The Phone Call

Sunday, 30 December 2018
06h05

The harsh ringing of a phone abruptly ends an awful nightmare. As I tear open my sleep-encrusted eyelids, I'm grateful it's only been a bad dream. I realise my phone is buzzing on the bedside table next to me, and I reach over anxiously. Early morning calls never bring good news.

I see 'Didi' – my sister's pet name – and the three familiar love hearts on the screen. At two years old, my daughter, Daniella, had called her Didi because Cindy was impossible to pronounce. Ironically, it means 'sister' in Hindi.

How strange, I think. *Cindy is in the Hunter Valley with a couple of girlfriends for the New Year's weekend, and besides, she never calls me this early in the morning.*

'Hello? Cindy?' I croak.

'Lisa,' she says breathlessly, 'Ralph can't get hold of

Daddy – no-one can. He isn't answering his phone. The security company is also looking for him because he didn't set the alarm at work. Milo is in the house, barking. The house is all locked up and it's dark.'

She is filled with panic. It unsettles me, and I feel my heart racing wildly.

'What do you mean no-one can get hold of him?'

I suddenly remember my terrible nightmare, but I don't dare tell my sister. In my dream, my father had shot himself because he found himself in desperate debt. It had been so vivid that when I opened my eyes to the sound of the phone ringing, I momentarily imagined it was true. Now I try to steady myself and remain calm as my training as a psychiatrist has taught me to do.

'When did anyone last see Dad?'

Cindy isn't sure. All she knows is that the security company to which Dad's work alarm is linked, rang our younger brother, Ralph, because Dad hasn't done what he usually does – set the security alarm at his car yard at 1pm on a Saturday. This is highly unusual behaviour – Dad is never shoddy about this sort of thing.

For the past few years, Dad has run a humble used-car business in a small country town, Worcester, an hour's drive from Cape Town in South Africa, the city of my birth. It's a pretty sad operation, if I'm being honest. In reality, the car yard is a fenced-off gravel area with two wooden huts, a few second-hand cars – mainly utes (known as 'bakkies' in South Africa) – and a separately placed large workshop with a tiny office, kitchenette and bathroom off of it. The car yard and workshop are one of a few unlucrative businesses that share the larger gravel area surrounded partially by brick walls and, in parts, only barbed-wire fencing because in South Africa, safety is paramount.

Cindy recounts again all the ways in which Dad is untraceable. He isn't answering his phone. It's 9pm in South Africa and 6am in Sydney, Australia, where my sister and I both live now. Dad is obsessed with his precious dog, Milo, and would *never* leave him alone in the dark. As a homebody, Dad loves to spend his Saturday afternoons relaxing on the couch with Milo, watching sport on television and snacking on biltong, cured dried meat, a staple in South Africa. Cindy has already spoken to Mike, his closest friend, but he too has no idea where Dad is even after inspecting the work premises.

Apparently, Mike says everything looks normal – all the cars are there, and nothing indicates a break-and-enter. Piet, Dad's watchman, is also on the premises. Dad feels sorry for him and keeps him employed to 'keep watch' over the vehicles; but in reality, all Piet does is sit in one of the wooden huts overnight, usually in a drunken sleep. Dad's routine on a Saturday is to leave by 1pm, go home and relax with Milo. Then he returns at 4pm to let Piet into the premises and give him a dinner of sandwiches and soup in winter.

Supposedly, Piet said he saw Dad earlier, but that's as much as he has divulged. Mike has, by all accounts, also checked Dad's home and reports that the house is dark and locked up. On top of that, Dad's scooter isn't at home or at work.

All these details are beginning to paint a troubling picture. Despite my training, my mind is beginning to spin.

Where could Dad be? He wouldn't be out. Maybe he is partying somewhere. But Dad doesn't ever go out. This is just wishful thinking. And if he did, he definitely wouldn't leave Milo at home in the dark. Plus, his only real friend is Mike, so who or where could he be if he isn't with Mike?

Suddenly, fear takes hold of me; and a cold river of panic gushes through my body, triggering the perceptible pounding of my heart. My skin is clammy and electric, as if there is a chemical reaction happening between my sweat glands and the invisible subcutaneous nerves and blood-fuelled vessels. I feel hot; but inside my head, my brain is frozen in fright. I find it impossible to have any clear thought. I suddenly imagine the worst.

Please, no. Oh my god, no!

I take a deep breath.

'I am going to try calling Dad. Hopefully, he answers. And I'll call Ralph. I will call you back. I need to find out what is happening. I love you.'

'I love you too,' Cindy says as we end the call.

Everything is quiet as I hold the phone to my ear. *I love my family and need to sort this out.*

I feel the walls getting closer, as if they're squashing me. My body and mind begin to uncouple, and I feel numb and stuporous as an expansive black void engulfs me.

Wait. Breathe. Stay calm, Lisa.

I gather myself enough to pick up my phone and ring Dad's number three times over. I feel certain he will pick up and say, 'Hello, Lisa, are you okay? Why are you calling me so early?' and straightaway, he will dissolve this moment of terror; but his phone keeps ringing out to voicemail. I hear Dad's familiar voice message, and it's deafening in my ears – 'This is Sam. I am not available. Please leave a message and I'll call you back.'

I don't want a call back – I want you to answer me now! Why aren't you answering? Dad, answer me now!

Fear and anxiety catapult me from my bed, down the long hallway from my bedroom to the front door and out the apartment. I walk briskly down the garden path beyond the driveway, all the way to the sidewalk so that Mum won't overhear me speaking. She has been staying with me in Sydney for the past two months, helping with my children, Daniella who is twelve and Rachel who is ten. Mum is always willing to pick up her life and be away from her home, Dad and Milo even for extended periods even though I know it's hard for her.

Dad, on the other hand, enjoys his alone time, whilst I 'babysit' Mum. I have come to prefer having my parents visit separately, and because I finance all these trips, I get to call the shots. It allows me more quality time with each parent; but mostly, I'm spared having to listen to their relentless, forty-year-marriage bickering which has tarnished prior visits as it did all through my childhood.

As I stand outside, I need to locate my contact list, but I'm struggling. My brain is registering threat, which is circulating adrenaline to my limbs. My tremoring fingers feel webbed, shaky and clumsy, causing me to fumble over the numbers. My mind is looping over the same thoughts. *I'm not ready for this. No, please, not now. Please, not Daddy. Please, God, please. I promise to do everything and anything You want from me. Please hear me and help me, only this once. I'll never ask again.*

I can't stop wishing to wake from this bad dream.

Please be a dream.

'Myers, David' – I find the number and dial. My dad's brother answers, but I'm suddenly aphasic, and I stumble over an easy phrase: 'Uncle David.' I manage two words between dread and tears. 'My dad is missing.'

'Talk to Diana,' he says. My aunt takes over the call.

'Lisa, what's wrong?" she asks with concern, infected by the tone of David's three words to me.

'Aunty Diana, my dad is missing.' Again, struggling to speak clearly, I pace up and down the pavement outside my house, sobbing. *Why? Why? Why? This can't be true. Please, please don't be true.*

'Oh my god, what do you mean?' Her question is a shriek of disbelief. Her distress scares me. I don't like it. Her reaction authenticates the overpowering and agonizing nervousness spreading like a plague through my body. *Why can't you be positive and say it's all okay?*

I recount what I know to my aunt. Aunty Diana is speechless as she absorbs and processes the information. *Aunty Diana always knows what to do and how to help.* But it's becoming unnervingly clear that she is helpless in finding my dad, and despite being miles away, her every emotion is like the blow of a boxer to my stomach. My mind is foggy. I desperately want Aunty Diana to ease my anxiety, but we both know my dad and the details thus far are undeniably foreboding.

07h12

Pacing the pavement, I call Mike. I tell him I'm worried.

'I am worried too.' Mike's deep voice and his melodic

slow and calm tone are like a comforting, familiar embrace. Mike is kind, caring and loyal, and there is sincere concern in his address. *I know Mike will help find Dad.*

'Lisa, I am sorry, but it isn't clear what has happened to your Dad,' Mike says.

'When did you last talk to him?' I interrupt.

'A while back. I've been away,' his tone is apologetic.

I beg Mike to help. Each passing second adds another layer to my rapidly rising panic. Mike agrees to drive past the family home and Dad's business premises again, in the hope of finding additional clues. I know Mike wants to help, but he doesn't seem infected with my urgency, and this annoys me. Mike cares, but maybe not enough or maybe he feels helpless or doesn't think Dad's disappearance is a problem. Frustrated by Mike's inability to fix this problem, I hang up the phone and dial my brother, Ralph, who has spoken to someone at the security company. I pray he has more to offer.

07h31

'Ralph, this isn't good. When did you talk to Dad last?' I ask.

'I think yesterday or the day before. He was happy about seeing the grandchildren. I told him I was coming to Worcester for New Year's with Ethan and Sadie.'

'What can we do?'

'It's already 10.30pm here. I don't know what else I can do.'

'Ralph, you need to drive to Worcester. You have to go and look for Dad. Go and check the hospitals, call the police, check the roads and look for his scooter. He might have fallen. I spoke to Mike and asked him to go and check the house and at Dad's work again. Please, Ralph, I am so stressed. Something has happened to Daddy. Call me when you get to Worcester, okay?'

'Okay, I'll go now.' His words are heavily laden with responsibility. All our hopes for Dad's wellbeing rest on him. It's up to Ralph to find Dad.

'And Ralph, I haven't told Mommy. She can't know about Dad yet.'

As I stand in the driveway, I think about how I have to shield Mum from this news as long as possible. My role as her protector is not new. I have been looking after my mother all my life. She lost both her parents and her baby sister tragically and very young. She has never quite recovered, and my dad is her rock. Mum is anxious and overwhelmed by the slightest stress.

I call Cindy to update her on the last two hours of frantic, but seemingly useless conversations. We talk about Dad and hypothesise about his whereabouts and the ridiculous concept of him lying dead somewhere. Talking to my sister about our father feels comforting because waiting and not knowing is agonizing. I feel so helpless. *If only I were in South Africa right now, I could find Dad.*

Above this, an incessant regret won't leave me:
I wish I had called Dad yesterday.

08h05

Back inside my house, I lay my head on my partner Jason's chest and form a wet blob on his t-shirt with my falling tears. My sobbing muffles my words as I recount the jumbled, second-hand stories about Dad.

'It will be okay. I promise you.' Jason's face is a mix of worry and care.

'I can't tell my mother – she will freak.'

'No, you can't,' Jason agrees. 'Not until you know what is happening. It might be unnecessary to worry her.'

'A cup of tea might be good and help you relax,' Jason offers. I make my way to the kitchen and then Mum walks in sheepishly.

'Morning, Lisa. How did you sleep?' she asks, checking my mood as she does every day.

I look at Mum, dressed in her baggy pyjamas, smiling back at me. 'I'm okay. I mean, I slept okay.'

She looks at me quizzically. 'You look upset.'

'I'm fine.' I try to discourage any further probing, but Mum's intuition is accurate.

'I can see you have been crying. Why? What's wrong? Has someone or something upset you?' Mum won't give up.

'No, I'm fine. I promise you. Nothing has happened. I am okay. Do you want tea?'

'Yes, please,' Mum says. I try to avoid any conversation, so I keep my focus on the scratched kitchen counter and the seemingly complex task of making a cup of tea.

'Lisa, please don't let anyone or anything bother you. You are an amazing person.'

I know where she's coming from with her uplifting maternal positivity, but she doesn't know what we are all potentially facing. Everything has its limits. Her optimistic statements are well intended, but nothing Mum can say will pick me up. Little does she know, I am – as usual – in the maternal role here, protecting her.

'We are going shopping for furniture soon. Come with us.' I don't want her to be alone, but also, my own abandonment anxiety of not knowing where Dad is makes me want to keep Mum close. I have an intense urge to cling tightly to her like a mother protecting her babies. I need her within tactile and visual range at all times.

My poor mother.

09h06

My phone rings again. *Please be Dad. Or someone offering relieving, good news.*

It's Ralph.

'Lisa, I've arrived in Worcester. Chantelle, me and the kids. We went to Eben Donges Hospital and Mediclinic, but neither have record of anyone fitting Dad's profile. They haven't had anyone brought in tonight, but they have my details and will call if they do. We drove around everywhere, but no sign of his scooter, or him. Nothing. Then we went to the police to file a missing person's. They hadn't heard anything and have no reports of accidents or any other incidents. Nothing. But they took details and said they would look into it.'

I try to absorb this news. 'What does that mean? Can't they do more? Can't they go search for him?' I'm frustrated and angry.

'It's early days. He hasn't been gone long enough. They said they will drive around and see, and go to the premises and the house. But we were at the house earlier, and there was nothing. Milo was there, but otherwise, we couldn't see or find anything. Only Dad's phone was there, charging on the kitchen table. We have that now and will keep it. Also, there was one empty glass in the sink. We're going back to the house now. The kids are asleep in the car. It's one in the morning here.'

I hear the exhaustion in his voice, but still, I need answers.

10h13

I feel numb inside. Like a ghost, I walk around Moore Park shopping centre with Mum, Jason and Rachel, who is irritable and cranky. Rachel must sense my fear and anxiety, and she tries to get me to be my usual, present self.

'Why are you getting so many phone calls?' Mum asks suspiciously. 'Why are you walking away to talk? What are you hiding?'

'Nothing. It's just my work stuff,' I say, trying to be nonchalant. But my façade is crumbling.

Cindy calls and then Diana rings too for a progress report, but I only have Ralph's scanty information to give. Time passes slowly, and each tiny movement of the second hand on my wristwatch seems indirectly proportional to my escalating despondency. *This isn't good. Deep down, I know Dad isn't okay. This is just too out of the ordinary for him.*

Rachel throws herself onto the floor trying to get my attention, but I'm torn between phone calls and salespeople showing me a range of couches. I can't be empathetic to Rachel right now because in this hyper-aroused state, my frustration tolerance is low. I know she needs me, but I'm trying to manage my anxiety and I have nothing to give her. I feel disorientated, trying zealously to be an ordinary shopper: browsing, touching, thinking, deciding and paying. I keep trying to pretend nothing is wrong and allow denial to take over.

'Wow, I love all these things I bought. I can't wait to see them in the house. The couch will look spectacular!' For a fleeting moment, I'm free from the grip of torment.

'I don't think I've ever bought so many things in such a short space of time! And such big things at that!' I laugh. Mum and Jason chuckle too. *Perhaps my fretting has been a waste of time? Maybe Dad is fine, and one day, I'll reflect on this and the absurdity of worrying?* I want to be furious at Dad for causing this anguish because he foolishly fell asleep on a couch in a random person's home and didn't have his phone and couldn't drive because he had one-too-many whiskeys.

I'm scrambling, scrounging at improbables and I know it.

11h11

At home, we all help unpack the car. My phone rings again. It's Ralph. Please let him be calling to say *he's found Dad!*

'Lisa,' I note the exhaustion in his voice, 'it's two in the morning. I am very tired. I've got such a painful headache.

I haven't slept for almost two days because I came off an overnight stock take and haven't slept yet. My head is pounding. The kids are asleep in Mum and Dad's bed, and Chantelle is here with me. We are going to bed. I will get up at five and try again. Maybe in the light, we will see more and find Dad…or something.'

'Of course, Ralph. Thanks for everything. Go to sleep. I will talk to you in a few hours.' I try to sound supportive, but I'm crushed with despondency. The day has been a marathon, leaving me worn-out and sick to my stomach with the gnawing sensation of doom. Mum sits, naively watching a show on TV. My heart plunges, and I feel tears build. I turn and leave the room. I want Mum to rest. *In three hours' time, I will phone Bear. Bear works with Dad and has for many years. He knows all Dad's coming and goings. Bear will know where Dad is.*

14h08

'Bear, my dad is missing. Ralph is at home. Please, you need to help. Please, Bear. Something is wrong with my dad. Go get Ralph and see if you can find my dad,' I beg into the phone.

'Ja, okay, Lisa. *Ek doen so,*' he replies in Afrikaans, assuring me he will do what he can.

I am crying uncontrollably, and this seems to make Bear nervous. He sounds panicked. *Why is he worried? Does Bear know something? Why doesn't he have a plausible explanation for Dad's disappearance? Bear knows Dad so well.*

14h49

'Mum, I've got this parenting video being filmed tomorrow, so I'm going to get my hair done.' Knowing Ralph and Bear have left to find Dad, I go about my day. I have to prepare for work tomorrow, and Dad's pending misadventure has taken enough of my time.

'Okay, see you soon. Enjoy!' Mum chirps in reply.

I get into the front passenger side of the car and Jason, the driver's side. We sit silently, thinking about the past nine long hours. We still have no news.

My phone rings for the umpteenth time – it's Ralph again.

I am not prepared for the sound of Ralph wailing and gasping for air. His cries and screams cut into me. I hear him say my name. *I don't want to hear more.* My heart is galloping.

'Lisa...' My baby brother cries out my name a second time.

'Lisa...' I want to help him, hold him and comfort him, but I can't; and he can't articulate more than a single word. I am floating, and the world around me seems unreal. Finally, I hear his agonizing cry across the Indian Ocean, and the words I pleaded never to receive reverberate like crashing thunder in my ears.

'Lisa, they've cut him up! They've cut Daddy up!'

CHAPTER 2

My Journey

That devastating phone call was the starting pistol that marked the beginning of my journey of trauma and mourning.

My father's death upended and changed my life forever. Everything fell apart the day he died, throwing me into confusion and emotionally eviscerating me.

For the first time, I knew firsthand what it meant to have symptoms of post-traumatic stress disorder (PTSD) combined with grief. In the months following his death, I suffered from jumbled thoughts, flashbacks, frequent nightmares and strange visual illusions of imaginary dark shadows. I was disconnected from the world, as if living in a bubble from which I could see out, but no-one could see in. The world seemed strange, pointless and rushed; and although I was alive, I was not living. I felt depressed and paralysed as I floated around, isolated in my snow-globe world, whilst from the outside, people saw me functioning and coping. It's difficult to completely understand experiences you haven't lived. I can admit now that prior to my father's death, I had been clueless and thoughtless towards those mourning the loss of a parent.

I am still not sure how, but I have survived the initial trauma and am working my way through the never-ending process of grieving. But I still have been unable to get any answers as to how and why my father died. Despite my tenacity, I have been forced to let it go without the closure I so desperately need. It has left me deflated to agonise over my efforts, wondering if I did enough.

Although my story is shocking and, at times, gruesome, it is by no means the worst experience in the expanse of human suffering. I don't want to be pitied or regarded as a noble victim of psychological pain or to cause you, my reader, any vicarious trauma. I share it and the hard-won meaning I have made from it, in the hope that it might help you to navigate your own path through your trauma.

In the upcoming chapters, I will share the details of my father's death and the investigation I pursued after the authorities in South Africa deemed it a suicide and shut the case – this was part of my own healing process. Please navigate these pages with caution. The specifics are shocking and belong more in an episode of CSI than in anyone's life. I have included these terrible details after careful consideration. Narrating my story tamed the ghastly nature of my trauma by providing safe re-exposure and giving time to befriend the responses of my body and mind. Peeling away the layers of trauma has revealed the depth of grief, which I've learnt is an endless, winding road.

Trauma is threaded through everyone's life, but on a

spectrum, it extends from the micro-fractures of a mother rejecting her child, to the macro and gross violations of abuse and neglect. I, like everyone else, have experienced trauma of varying degrees peppered through my life, beginning with my mother whose own traumas left her emotionally unavailable. My parents had a difficult marriage, and their arguments echoed throughout my childhood, leaving me confused about love and afraid of abandonment. My teens were fraught with shame and extreme perfectionist behaviours. I then struggled with postnatal depression (PND), and my marriage ended in divorce, leaving my children forever pained at not having a 'normal' family (if there is such a beast). These were nothing compared to the trauma that awaited me when my father died.

I grew up in a family surrounded by people struggling with mental health issues. I went on to study medicine in Stellenbosch, followed by psychiatry in Johannesburg. Much to my father's dismay, I eventually qualified as a psychiatrist. In arguments with Dad, he'd often retort, 'All psychiatrists are crazy,' to which I'd respond that he had made me; and so, by default, he must be crazy too. My father was devoutly non-judgemental (except about psychiatrists) and taught me not to be critical of others. I'm grateful to have the opportunity daily to honour his life philosophy through my work, where I meet every client where they are, with an open heart and without judgement.

This book forms part of my father's legacy. Writing those words both comforts and pains me. Processing the shock surrounding his death has helped me find the words to narrate this story.

But many trauma sufferers don't have the language to articulate their experiences which remain deeply and subconsciously embedded in their brains. They are expressed non-verbally via random, disjointed and uncomfortable physical sensations, painful emotions, distressing thoughts and mental images. These symptoms are often not identified as being part of the trauma or sometimes misdiagnosed as a separate condition when a clinician is focused predominantly on the presenting features rather than the background story. Underlying trauma can be overlooked because people don't always consciously remember it, or are too ashamed to disclose intimate details to a stranger.

Trauma can present with an array of non-specific and overlapping symptoms with other mental health diagnoses. For instance, someone with a depressed mood, disturbed sleep and self-loathing might be diagnosed with a major depressive disorder. Another suffering hyperarousal, inattention and restlessness might attract an ADHD diagnosis; and their distrust, dissociation, numbing and self-harming behaviour might be explained as a personality disorder. Even if these diagnostic labels are correctly assigned, my experience is that failing to recognise and treat the underlying trauma results in poor immediate and long-term improvements.

When assigning a diagnosis, psychiatrists follow the Diagnostic and Statistical Manual-V (DSM-V), which has evolved over the years and is currently in its fifth edition. It is a categorical classification system that gives a particular diagnosis when a cluster of certain symptoms are present together with significant distress and functional impairments in various areas of life. It provides clinicians with a universal system and a common language with which to communicate their mutual understanding of a patient who presents with certain symptoms. Essentially, it justifies treatment costs to health-care agencies and insurance companies. While this can be helpful, the manual does not specify causality – in other words, what has caused these symptoms to present themselves in the first place.

Aetiology (or the study of causes) is, you may be surprised to learn, not a pre-requisite in making a diagnosis. For example, while many people will be diagnosed with depression, none of them will have the same underlying causative factors. Failing to discover and help a patient heal from this primary wound, I believe, is a missed opportunity to help a patient get well. Sadly, with the DSM-V's primary focus on symptoms and the allocation of a diagnostic label, many individual stories of human suffering are lost as they dissolve into the bolus of criteria needed to fit a DSM-V diagnosis.

In my work, I try to help my clients navigate and heal their deep-set, painful life experiences which have caused their suffering while together we manage their presenting mental health issues.

We all have painful stories to overcome, and it's important to remember that it is never a competition about who has suffered worse or more. On the relative nature of grief, Mark Twain eloquently said, 'Nothing that grieves us can be called little: by the eternal laws of proportion a child's loss of a doll and a king's loss of a crown are events of the same size.' What is important is that we each acknowledge our suffering. We do this by owning it, and from that moment on, we can begin to change.

I have long wished to write a book about mental health and share my journey of growth and development. I want to normalise the struggles we all have with mental health and reduce the stigma which obstructs people from accessing help. I've had the benefits of long-term therapy and have made it my life's work to understand this area and how it's possible to rewire the brain and change one's life. I want to share what I know to empower you to do the same.

I had already begun writing this book when my father died under horrific circumstances. That, of course, wasn't my plan. But it forced me to step away and rediscover myself without a father, and incorporate my mourning into this book. In the wake of this loss, I needed time to piece my life together again. That is what trauma does – it creates a bitsy narrative because a frightened mind cannot be present enough to process and integrate a complete experience. I know this because I have studied trauma. I've read numerous books on the topic, heard about how it hijacks human life from frightened clients, discussed these cases with colleagues and witnessed its multiple manifestations during my training as a doctor and psychiatrist.

Before my own experience of it, I was fairly well versed in trauma theory – the structural and functional damage it causes to the brain's biology, and the negative impact on cognitive development. It wages war on a person's self-formation, their sense of being lovable and worthy of care, and it shatters basic trust in the world and the idea that relationships can be good and safe. I had a sufficient understanding of trauma prior to my father's death, but losing him in the most gut-wrenching way forced me to live it. I have been made to see this as a gift that I need to take into my work for the benefit of others.

While exploring the chapters of my life story, I have grown in my ability to choose how to live going forward even though I am not in control of what lies ahead. In the process, I have gained greater understanding of myself and a deeper awareness of my emotions. I now consciously decide the path I want to walk. At a biological level, I am forming new neuronal pathways. I am using therapy to shape my brain to be mindful, measured, thoughtful, contextual, positive and accepting. I have changed and feel more in control over many aspects of my existence. Despite all this, I continue to stumble over my many psychological blind spots, which I still need to acknowledge and develop the courage to overcome.

It was my father who taught me: *life is your lesson*. I've repeated this to many clients since. Losing Dad forced me to confront many new lessons, but I am still learning. Fortunately, I've been able to examine and reflect on my trauma through my psychiatrist's lens. My regret and lack of closure have undoubtedly been the most challenging aspects of my loss. The upside is that my father's death has brought me greater compassion and understanding. Life always gives us a chance to grow even if we don't like the lessons.

But I am not glamorising or romanticising suffering that leads to psychological growth. We all have to learn to accept our lives as they unfold, and to make meaning from it all.

As a therapist, I come from the position that relationships help us heal – it is in relationships that we build our sense of self, so it follows logically that any rebuilding of self equally requires a good relationship. I didn't have perfect parents (Who does?) nor have I had perfect relationships (there aren't any). But it is through both good and bad that we shape ourselves and become who we are, and later, who we choose to be.

My relationship with my father transitioned over the years from idealising him to questioning him. But I had enough of a secure foundation and attachment on which to build my daily practice of helping other people along their journey of wellness. We're all largely products of our parents. Their nature and nurture influences mould our personalities though, of course, there are many other factors that contribute to shaping our development.

I attribute the unique qualities I bring to my job to the quirks of my personality and upbringing. I often find myself repeating statements that I heard from my father over the years, and as I go about my day, I sometimes visualise him sitting on my shoulder or hear his comforting voice inside me. It's important to me that my clients find me both real and authentic.

As a doctor, I am trained in mental health, which requires daily attention – just like physical health. We naturally attend to our bodies, whether it be treating illness, minor ailments or tweaking what has been transcribed by our genetic code. We all understand the imperatives of maintaining a healthy diet and doing regular exercise to manage hypertension, diabetes and excess weight. But somehow, we don't get that the same vigilance applies to our mental health. There still seems to be a stigma that managing our mental health means we are sick in the head, crazy or 'nuts.' Carrying a bit too much weight doesn't appear as shameful as having borderline personality traits or being on the autistic spectrum. We are quicker to judge variances in mental health than we are with physical health.

I wrote this book because I am passionate about good mental health, and I want to help others manage theirs. In helping others, we help ourselves. This has proved true for me.

Unfortunately, psychiatry has always been the ugly sister of the medical family. It has a chequered history characterised by strait jackets, asylums, shock therapy, overmedication, pills to treat illness, pills to treat side effects of the pills to treat the illness, forced injections, padded cells, sedation, restraints, policemen, scheduling and involuntary admissions. Too often, people are misdiagnosed, given multiple diagnoses or no diagnosis at all, which detracts from the credibility of psychiatry as a field. Mental health practitioners would readily agree that psychiatry is both a science and an art, as differences in interpretation make up the colours of subjectivity in any client's assessment and formulation. Scientology groups, amongst others, refer to it as 'unreal' and 'torturous,' going as far as blaming psychiatrists for terrorism because it alters peoples' minds.

Fear is incited when the mentally ill are depicted as impulsive, unpredictable and violent. Movies such as *Girl Interrupted* and *One Flew Over the Cuckoo's Nest* have not helped the cause. Celebrities undergoing personal challenges, such as Britney Spears and Caitlyn Jenner, have been used by the media to gain viewership by sensationalising particular aspects of mental health. The list of negative associations goes on and on, making it almost impossible for helpful messages about mental health to get through to the ordinary person as a site of personal growth where trust, engagement and ultimately, healing and wellness can be found.

Sadly, I have experienced rejection from colleagues working in other disciplines within the medical fraternity, who have snubbed my speciality as 'not really medicine' and shown similar disrespect and disdain to my clients.

I've entered overfull emergency departments only to be told by an annoyed doctor, pointing to a distressed (often disruptive) client, saying, 'That's yours! It's been a nightmare for the past twelve hours. They've been screaming and swearing, and tearing their clothes off. We are full here. Would you make a plan to sort them out?'

It? (As if they are not human.) *Sort them out?* (As if there's a simple pill to switch the problem off.)

Leaving an unattended pot to boil is never a good idea. So, it's not surprising that the mental health tsunami has finally caused enough devastation to escalate its significance and make it core business and an equal to its physical health brother (or sister, or non-binary sibling).

More people are presenting with mental health challenges in the past few years, and as a result, awareness of its prevalence is mushrooming. Suddenly, it's on the agenda everywhere – in parliament, offices, workplaces and schools. We talk about it at the dinner table. Celebrities openly share their battles with mental health and endorse the view of vulnerability being a source of greater inner strength. It is no longer taboo for people to share that they suffer from anxiety and depression. Help is readily advertised as is the encouragement to accept it. While progress has been remarkable, we still have craters to explore, navigate and explain the range of normalcy to pathology. When we eventually understand mental health (and mental illness), we will pave the pathway to change. This book is my contribution to this conversation.

As the expert, people expect me to have all the answers to all the questions. They think of me as perfect and without any problems. But I don't and I am not, because not only do I treat mental health, I have to work on maintaining my own too. Though I don't have my life seamlessly put together, on most days, it is good enough. I am grateful that psychiatry has evolved to the point where therapists can be more vulnerable, approachable and real.

I invite you to walk with me on my journey of trauma, grief and self-discovery. I hope you will make space for curiosity to replace judgement, and let yourself expand beyond the knowns, deeply into your conscious and unconscious mind. Perhaps you might like to make notes of your feelings, thoughts and urges as you read. You could even keep a journal if that helps. If you become unsettled or feel distress, please seek additional support. I have done my best to hold you within the pages of this book, but you may need more. In my life and work, I have touched and been touched by the lives of many other trauma sufferers who have shone a light in my darkest hours.

I hope that in sharing my journey, you will be inspired to reflect, think, feel, heal and grow.

CHAPTER 3

The Bearer of Bad News

As my brother's words and cries ripped right through me, I had never experienced such intense pain. In that moment, I froze. I knew I was supposed to cry, but I couldn't.

Did this mean I didn't care? I felt an uncomfortable urge to laugh. *Why? How was this funny?* Finally, I felt a cry, a dreadful scream, leave my throat. I heard those guttural sounds as if they were coming from someone else, but it was me.

I don't remember ending the phone call with my brother, but I do recall thinking: *I have to tell my sister, and then my mother.*

In moments of strife, my family has always come together. My parents always modelled and encouraged forgiveness and unconditional love, so when faced with a shared challenge, we easily dispelled arguments and differences. 'She's your sister' and 'he's your brother' were sufficient reasons for us to abandon resentments and anger towards one another.

I had to let Cindy know. Reluctantly, I pressed the keys on my phone.

'Cindy,' I paused, 'Ralph found Daddy. He's dead. He's been cut up. They killed him.'

We were both stunned into muteness as my words sunk in.

Her sobs of disbelief hurt me and I began to tremble. I didn't know how to comfort my older sister, who couldn't be more different from me. If I am determined, fastidious and to-the-point, she is free-spirited, indecisive and intuitive. She represents stability and reliability to me because she has always been a constant in my life. My sister never had children of her own but has been a second mother to my daughters. Visualising her bent over and gasping, I felt my emotions pour out, and the two of us wept into the reality that our family was now broken forever.

The only facts I knew were that Ralph had found Dad semi-naked on the cold concrete floor of his workshop covered in blood. According to Ralph, he had been butchered or even tortured. There was no doubt that he had suffered. Though the story was patchy and jumbled, it appeared from what Ralph had seen of Dad's body and the bloodshed, that he had been murdered.

How would he live with the image of our father's body, cold and lifeless, in his own blood?

But my anxiety about how Ralph would cope had to wait.

It was time to tell my poor mother. She was not a stranger to trauma, having lost many of her family members under awful circumstances. Mum is the perfect blend of resilience and fragility, yet no amount of inner strength could prepare her for what I was about to tell her. I didn't want to expose my children to what I imagined would be a shattering response, so I called my ex-husband Steven and asked him to collect them.

Steven and Dad had had a father-son type relationship. When my parents visited, Steven and Dad had enjoyed watching sports on TV, having a beer and sharing silly dad jokes together. Steven had always admired my father's dedication to family. Their relationship had survived the end of our marriage, and Steven still loved and respected my father.

'I'm so sorry, Lisa,' he whispered as he took Rachel out. She waved innocently from the car and smiled. My smile back to her was the last of a life that would never be the same again.

As I turned back, Mum approached me at the front door with a look that told me she knew something terrible had happened.

'Mum,' I began, 'I have to tell you something.' It was all she needed to hear. Her tears came fast. There was such fear and knowing in her wide eyes.

'Oh, no, please...' My mother knew me well – she birthed and raised me and could read my face.

I'd seen movies like this, where the characters share moments of unimaginable shock and tragedy as they deliver bad news, but I was unprepared for being inside a real-life scene. What could I say that would help her make sense of Dad's death and support her manage this madness? I could barely comprehend it myself.

As I edged closer to her, I started crying too. 'Mommy....' It hurt knowing that my words would puncture my mother's already deeply tortured soul.

She looked at me and just yelled out, 'Please, no, no. What's happening?'

'Daddy's dead.'

And then, I watched my mother collapse to the floor and sob.

CHAPTER 4

Fight and Flight

'Would you like something to eat?'

I looked up at the airhostess towering over me, waiting for my response. But I had disassociated – my mind was a million miles away – as I typed away furiously on my Facebook profile, my fingers frustratingly slow. I found myself having to cope not only with the shock of my dad's death, but the way his death was being spoken about by family members who were convinced it was suicide. This outraged me. I felt responsible for protecting my father now that he could no longer do it himself.

The preceding forty-eight hours had been frantic as we tried to gather any bits of information, speaking to police and family, entertaining numerous visitors offering support, consoling each other, attempting to rationalise the obscure nature of events and struggling furiously to secure last-minute flights to South Africa. I was tired, but it was impossible to relax or rest. My body was in the height of sympathetic, flight mode and adrenaline pumped like oil from a well out of my adrenals.

During this time, I was experiencing a typical response to shock. Confronted with horror, I'd lost all perspective because the part of my brain – the limbic system – responsible for emotions was 'interfering' with the parts (dorsolateral and medial frontal lobes) governing rationality and internal awareness and tolerance of stress. In such moments, the important functions of our frontal lobes, like good judgement and thoughtful decision-making ability, become warped by the neurological force of intense emotions – as does our ability to accurately gauge stress, resulting in hyper-arousal and intensified reactivity. Stress and trauma overload our regular filters, making everything within and around us appear overwhelming and triggering. While everyone responds differently, I was being pushed beyond my capacity to regulate emotion; and as the tension grew, I activated the 'release valve,' relieving the uncomfortable pressure of my feelings. Simply said, I had no self-control.

Reflecting now, I realise that my choice to vent on Facebook was not appropriate and was motivated by my need to vehemently defend my father, my family and myself. It was the only way to relieve my feelings of intense shame and anger. In the face of trauma, we often fight back from a place of past trauma. In my case, all the years of feeling like an outcast in our community as Jews made me defensive in this moment. I couldn't bear for Dad to be judged without his story being heard. And although it was irrelevant (Dad was dead, and rationally, I knew that the opinions of others were just that), I was defending every person impacted by the cruelty in the world (as I do in my work).

As my narcissistic defences grew Goliath-like, I muscled to gather support for Dad. I never entertained the thought that I might appear foolish or be proven wrong (not that our feelings can ever be considered wrong). I was acting on impulse to fence any judgement of my father and my family. I was hurt and ashamed of being 'different' and 'not good enough,' which was the curse of my childhood. I felt as if I'd been transported back to being a little girl. I perceived the entire world as cruel, unkind and judging.

From my seat, I caught a glimpse of Mum sitting across from me on the aisle. She looked ashen, her face scrunched in confused anguish, and her eyes glazy and red from endless crying. The ugly black eye she'd sustained from her hard fall after hearing the news about Dad stood out like the bull's eye on a dartboard. What a sight we must all have looked. Each of us took turns breaking down, in desperate competition for comfort, as we scrambled individually to express the personal impact of our loss. We all needed help.

'It will be okay,' I said, reluctantly placing a hand on my sister's back as she sat slumped over in a foetal-like position, regressed in terror, gasping for air. I knew she was panicked by feelings of abandonment. In her case, Dad's death triggered her fears of desertion and being unable to cope without him. I knew she needed reassurance, and I wanted to offer it, but I desperately needed comforting too. My resentment waxed and waned, and so too my ability to wrap my sister and mother in the warmth of a solacing embrace. *What about my grief?* We were all in a state of shock and ruled by our most primal instincts. Our actions were thoughtless, our bodies on autopilot, severed from reality and conscious decision-making. It became near impossible to hear or see each other's needs, not out of selfishness, but because we were detached, unable to be present and absorb what was needed of us. We each felt alone in our struggle.

Beyond survival, we were individually unleashing our trauma ogre. Dad's death had triggered a simultaneous firing of the multiplicity of traumas we had each suffered over our lives, individually and collectively, in our separately and at times, overlapping surrounding worlds. It had sparked a trauma auction, you could say – a bidding war for attention, each one calling out louder for any form of consolation for the excruciating pain. Trauma is like a thread that weaves its way through generations of individuals, spreading into the fabric of our being, instilling patterns of behaviour that underpin our traits and later solidifies lasting states. It creates the ties that bind us in beautiful bonds of empathy, but simultaneously enmeshes us in tangled attachments of collective misery and destruction. At times, our shared and individual trauma brings mutual kindness and combined strength, but we were like lions wrestling for a piece of meat.

In keeping with Jewish law, my father had to be buried as soon as possible. The Beth Din, the Jewish Rabbinical Court in South Africa, was adamant that a decision needed to be made: either we make our way to South Africa and bury Dad immediately, or we instruct that Dad's body not be released from the mortuary so that an autopsy could be done. We were pressured into a decision, and we decided to bury him.

The acuity of hindsight is tormenting. As I emerged from the trauma-blur months later, I realised how wrongly we acted. I deeply regret the decision to bury Dad without having a more detailed autopsy to conclusively determine the nature of his death. But without much choice, we buckled under the pressure to make a decision at a time when we were unable to make a rational and sensible one.

Human beings remember an event proportionally to the emotional intensity experienced at the time. However, we don't consciously and coherently recall all memory, which explains my fractured recollection of the conversation Mum, Cindy, Ralph and I had by phone whilst we waited at the airport in Johannesburg for the final leg of our journey to Cape Town. We allowed our beliefs of 'what Dad would have wanted' to steer the debate regarding the pros and cons of having a further autopsy done. Without much effort, we unanimously uttered Dad's familiar statements: 'Don't waste your time and money. It's not important. Get on with your lives. Take care of yourselves and each other. Don't worry about me.'

I'd planned to return to South Africa for only one week, completely unprepared for the unquantifiable distress ahead. In trying to control the uncontrollable, I negotiated terms with myself, and silently with Dad, and decided to set aside what felt like a reasonable amount of time away from my children and my clients, to whom I always feel a great sense of responsibility. One week. It seems laughable now.

I arrived in Cape Town, from Sydney, in what seemed

like minutes. I hadn't slept. We were met at the airport by my father's brother, Uncle David, and his daughter Sally. It was a sombre welcoming. As we emerged from the airport, the familiar lightness of South Africa already felt leaden and different. We immediately journeyed from the airport to my uncle's home. Soon after arriving, we briefed the Rabbi who would bury Dad the next day.

How would I communicate the memories of my life with my father in only a few hours? How would I do justice to the man Dad was? How would I brief the Rabbi, who didn't know Dad, enough to deliver the final message of his life and encapsulate his legacy?

All these thoughts were a jumble inside me as I clawed my way through these surreal hours.

CHAPTER 5

Losing Two Fathers

My father was one of four siblings, two of whom immigrated to America as young adults. Despite the feeling that our family bonds remained strong, I felt a void growing up without all our aunts, uncles and first cousins nearby. My father and Uncle David had stayed in South Africa. This was another reason, beyond their proximity in age, location and similar personality traits, that they were very close and why my siblings and I established affectionate bonds with our cousins that persisted into adulthood. Our cousins are both family and friends.

My Uncle David has always been like a second father to me and was my first point of call whenever I was in need. So, when I was sixteen and was accepted for a year-long exchange program in America, I found myself anxiously sitting in the car whilst Mum drove the hour-long journey from Worcester to Cape Town, where Uncle David lived.

Dad's words were still ringing in my ears. 'I'm so proud

of you, Lisa, but you will need to find the money – I don't have it.'

I grew up accepting that my father couldn't afford certain things. I often felt bereft and frustrated as he accounted for the necessities, but I was left to figure out how to afford any 'luxuries.' As an adult, I'm immensely thankful that this training made me stronger, more independent and grateful for what I have. It taught me how to work hard for whatever I want.

At sixteen I stood in the kitchen across from my Uncle David, he on one side of the counter and me on the other, with Mum close behind me. Their kitchen was full of the sights, smells and tastes of love. Standing there, I felt a sense of déjà vu as the countless family *shabbats* and Jewish festivals flashed through my mind – all the occasions in which my Aunty Diana's chicken soup and *kneidlach* (matzah balls) had simmered in a big silver pot on the old white stovetop. I put forward my request for money; and instantly, my eyes welled-up with tears, my legs tremored and my heart pounded. I felt small, but huge in shame, having to ask for his help. I distinctly remember thinking, *I never want to be in this position having to ask someone for money ever again.*

My uncle was gracious and kindly wrote a cheque for three thousand rand, which was a fortune of money at the time. Seeing how pathetic and frightened I was, he tried to lighten the mood and said with a joking smile, 'I won't be giving you such a big wedding present.'

Where is Dad? He insisted that I do this because he can't help me, so why isn't he here to support me?

I had stood woefully naked in my vulnerability, feeling

reduced to nothingness in my pleas for help. Thankfully, my uncle protected and supported me as did my mother who hugged me as I cried in my embarrassment and relief.

There were other such moments in my life when I'd leaned on my uncle and felt a close connection to him. He'd given a speech at my bat mitzvah when I was an awkward, frizzy-haired twelve-year-old girl, and the only Jewish one in my school and town of Worcester. I carried my religion around like a sack over my shoulder – cumbersome and unconcealable. On that day, the only synagogue in town was full of people – an unusual occurrence as all the Jews had left the smaller country towns by then, having moved to the cities or migrated overseas. I cried as my Uncle David spoke. At that stage, I already felt a strong bond with him, and his moving and meaningful words unlocked the pain I felt in my own family.

I had always held my aunt and uncle in high regard as they'd always been so supportive and caring over the years. But on this particular day, with my father's death still fresh in my heart, I was an outline of a person as I walked into their apartment. It was a place in which I had spent a number of memorable moments with my father, sitting around their dining room table, enjoying elaborate, delicious meals prepared by my aunt. I'd always felt warmth, happiness and togetherness in their home. On this trip, it would become my base during the following days of investigation and sorrow.

In Jewish culture, the period of mourning is called *shiva*. The name is literal. It's Hebrew, meaning 'seven,' and that's how many days members of the immediate family sit together – a form of meditation in itself – to reflect on the life of the loved one who has left. In Uncle David's apartment, I sat *shiva* with my mother, sister, brother, my father's three older siblings and other close relatives. It felt fitting to mourn my father in their home, as they had always felt like surrogate parents to me.

There were times when I was grateful for their presence as we shared conversations about my father. But because his death had been violent and no-one actually knew what had happened, I was also filled with frustration and anger.

When you're immersed in those first thick days of shock and sadness, you don't need the rules of an enforced religious period to make you focus on your grief. It already sticks to you like glue. But my *shiva* didn't provide a space and place for my feelings about what had happened to my father to evolve, because I was immediately consumed with the why and how of Dad's death. I began to examine the whole tragic catastrophe and everyone's mixed responses.

It was three days since my father's body had been found.

The grumblings of a potential suicide were now becoming the dark leitmotif in Dad's story. What? I was confused. Shocked. As my thoughts ran laps, I had no idea who or what to believe.

Family members began to utter flippant comments indicating they believed Dad had taken his own life. This cut me deeply. The worst part was that Uncle David was one of them. I felt not only that it was a betrayal of my dad, like the biblical brothers who turned their back on Joseph, but left me abandoned by my beloved and most respected uncle. *Did he have no faith in my father or at least realise how much I needed his support now more than ever?* For years, I'd revered his words as gospel, but now I was confused and weighed my truth against his opposing conviction. His statements felt cold and detached from the emotional impact of the tragedy, my father and our pain. Puzzled, I became paranoid that his responses were based on privy information about Dad's death that he could not or would not share with me.

Other family members understood my anger at these suggestions and took my side, reassuring me. Perhaps judging Uncle David was their way of honouring Dad. It was possibly easier for me to create a split between those who defended Dad and those who did not, than tolerate the messy multitude of mixed emotions everyone harboured and concealed about his death.

I didn't know what to make of my uncle's disconnected response, and I never found the right opportunity to raise it with him. In my pain, I did not give him the chance to explain his reaction or contemplate other possible explanations. I allowed my hurt and distrust to infuse the reality, and it caused me to misperceive his actions. The horrific nature of events touched all of us, causing communal bewilderment and varied inexplicable responses which were profound.

But after Dad died, I struggled to understand who my uncle was. At the time, I felt as if he'd not only been unkind to my dad, but to me too.

In time, I would have to grieve the loss not only of my father, but of my relationship with my uncle too.

CHAPTER 6
Thou Shalt Not Judge

One evening during the *shiva*, at the end of a long day of visitors, cups of tea, conversations about Dad, tears, hugs and countless offerings of 'I wish you long life,' I heard my Aunt Diana talking to her daughter Sally.

'You know, Mearl Abrahams said that for a long time, she'd noticed Sam looked depressed. He stopped coming to any of our functions, and he always seemed to have an excuse. And when he came, he didn't look happy.'

I went cold. *Who was this person, Mearl Abrahams, and why was she talking about my father? Why were any of them talking about my father? What gave her or any of them the right to judge his mental state and degree of depression or talk about it as if they were having a casual discussion about the latest bad movie they'd seen or substandard meal they'd had? Why was anyone talking about Dad when we were mourning, grappling with our loss, the trauma and brutality and the confusion?*

They were not psychologists or psychiatrists – yet

they had come to the conclusion that my dad had been depressed and suicidal. All because he hadn't attended functions or taken the long drive from Worcester to my aunt and uncle's holiday cottage in Churchhaven where they entertained their numerous friends by eating crayfish tails and sipping on expensive wines.

I became furious. I tried to speak, but I could only cry.

I wanted them to know the reasons – the *real* reasons – for Dad's lack of 'coming to the party' which they didn't know or think about. Sobbing and shaking, I managed to say, 'How dare you talk about my dad like this when you have no idea what he was going through or why he never came to your parties? My dad hated having to hear you and your friends talking about money, holidays, fancy restaurants, snobby connections and all the other superficial bullshit when he was struggling to pay the bills. He wasn't coming to Cape Town or Churchhaven because he didn't have the money to pay the petrol and the toll!'

How could they not see how it had made *him* feel? How did they not know that their invitations had only rubbed failure in his face and left him deflated? How could they not see that it wasn't about *them* and how *they* felt not having their gatherings attended? I felt betrayed and let down by those I'd considered our closest allies. Dad hated the superficial – as do I – especially when it undermines empathy and understanding of how others are suffering. Nothing makes me angrier than judgement of others without an adequate understanding of their full story.

'You'll never really understand a person until you consider things from his point of view. Until you climb inside of his skin and walk around in it.' As an impressionable sixteen-year-old, I'd read this quote in Harper Lee's *To Kill a Mockingbird*. Ever since then, it has guided me to always create a welcoming environment for vulnerable and exposed human beings shamefully seeking *any* relief from their torturous minds.

Dad's death triggered everyone's opinions, judgements and criticisms, which left me feeling personally attacked. As a result, my responses were extreme and uncurtailed. Dad's life had been a mixture of the unfair and the unwise. He had made poor choices at critical junctions in his life. Other times, his choices were simply not sensible. Sadly, on a number of occasions when life seemed to be looking up for him, another unfortunate setback happened once again, knocking him down. Many of the obstacles Dad faced were not unique to his life and cannot entirely account for the position he found himself in. I believe everyone deserves compassion because we are all different, and what is easy for some might be an incomprehensible challenge for another. Regardless, Dad's life story contained invisible pages that people couldn't see, and I found their external judgements and fault-finding narratives limited and prejudiced.

In the acuteness of the situation erupting around me, I allowed my interpretations of what was being said about Dad and the shame it evoked to influence my emotions and dictate my reactions. In many ways, I was the most condemnatory of other's judgements – how is that for irony?

The following morning, I walked into the apartment. The tension between me and my aunt was tangible.

'I'm sorry for my behaviour last night,' I said to her. 'I was upset and I over-reacted. I know you loved my dad, and I know that you are also hurting. I am just missing him, and I'm hurt and confused. It's all very hard to deal with, but thank you for opening your home to us and always being there. I am truly grateful.'

Diana gave me an understanding embrace. Over time, after Dad's death, she displayed growing compassion and regard for our grief. Her subliminal actions allowed my love and respect for her to grow as we re-established our connection. She was not my enemy. My displaced anger offered me some relief, but I had to acknowledge that I did not know my aunt's life's story and as such, was ill-equipped to critique her reaction. I am glad I was able to take ownership for my part, forgive her, and welcome her support and kindness with trust and gratitude when I needed it most.

In my grief, I was infuriated. Although, admittedly, it didn't take much to trigger my angry defence of my dad's honour. I can see now that I was also fighting to protect and rid my own shame by smearing it onto those around me. And perhaps, deep down, I was equally disappointed at my father's inability to manage his life.

Part of the reason everyone's judgements stung so deeply was because I'd already had such thoughts about my dad.

And I wasn't proud of them.

CHAPTER 7

The Heavy Burden of Shame

Dad had run a fabric business for many years while we were growing up, and although it had provided my father with enough money to raise a family, it wasn't ever a roaring success story. During the '90s, Dad's work life had transitioned into a role as a used-car salesman. I always avoided disclosing this because the truth is, I was ashamed. I had often heard used-car salesmen referred to as dodgy.

For many years of my adult life, my dad's dire financial situation had caused me ongoing stress and worry. My father was too kind to be a good businessperson. He'd always want to help and gave away more than he had. His generosity couldn't be planned and organised, qualities which are required when running a business. In fairness, he was always trying his best; but somehow, it seemed harder for him to be structured and have boundaries with others and himself. His good intentions would invariably fail to eventuate into returns. As a result, I often had to send money to help him out. From time to time, I'd fantasise about how much easier my life would be if Dad simply wasn't there needing my financial help to dig him out of his latest bad business decision. I am sad and filled with regret when I acknowledge this now. What was not much for me to give would have meant a lot to him. But even as I write this, it is important for you to know that I am not guilt-ridden.

As a psychiatrist, I know that thoughts are just that – thoughts – neurotransmitters along neurons and nothing else; my thoughts were not the cause of my dad's death. However, I have to live for the rest of my life with the truth that I had often hoped to live without my father's ongoing need for financial help and the burden it placed on me.

After years of coaching other people through their own guilt, I know better than to punish myself. We can't control our thoughts and feelings. They are all valid, and being human comes with being flawed. If I had been given the option to come to Dad's financial assistance and offer him the money he so clearly needed to help him survive, I would have done so in a flash. I never wanted his death or this pain, but I wasn't given the choice.

Over the years, I had struggled to set limits with my father when it came to lending money, but psychiatry had taught me to value setting good boundaries. I eased the guilt and overt responsibility I felt with justifications of preventing Dad's learnt helplessness and dependency.

'Psychiatry has changed you. It's made you hard,' Dad would sometimes say.

In relationships, when one person sets a boundary, it can often be interpreted as a lack of love or care; but the boundary I set with my father wasn't due to a lack of love. I'd convinced myself it was self-protective, but my inner child was angry and despondent for having spent years on the endless merry-go-round of giving, without him progressing.

After his death, regret knifed my heart and exceeded my guilt. I wish I'd spoken to Dad prior to his death and resolved the wedge in our closeness. On the surface, it was about his lack of money; but at the core, it represented my resentment, anger, disappointment and fear caused by years of feeling responsible for my parents. I never knew what might happen to them if I did not help them, and I had no experience of having my needs met in the expected parent-child dynamic on a consistent basis.

Since I'd been a child, I'd always been laden with the expectations to be more, give more and strive to be better. My conflicting emotions had been in a tug-of-war for many years and perhaps, might be for many more. It is impossibly hard to be responsible for a parent.

Every so often, I get to empathise with one of my young clients who finds themselves in a similar position. When your parents can't afford what other parents can because 'there just isn't enough money,' a battle ensues between the considerate and caring part of you, and your frustration and antipathy at their failings because of the burden it places on you.

I once sat opposite a young client who confessed, 'My friends don't know anything, and I don't want them to either. It's so embarrassing, but I understand my parents are trying their best and it could be worse. I can't make plans for next year like my friends because there just isn't enough money.'

She was tearful as she spoke about her family's recent financial collapse. I could resonate with her mixed emotions, her immense anxiety and her sadness at the loss of having her parents being able to care for her every need.

My dad's death and the aftermath tapped into so many of my insecurities. Was my father *good enough*? Was he someone I could feel proud of and respect? These were questions I had wrestled with for decades. They had always been dark places of deep shame, and now they were a confused mess of more shame tainted with anger and regret. I had always struggled with the feeling of my family being different and the ways those differences had made me feel embarrassed about who I really was.

My father had been an intelligent man and he had often spoken to me about how disappointed he was that he hadn't taken his education seriously and made more of his life. Perhaps it's why he always supported my obsessive studying habits and my dogged determination to be the best. I had a fearless pursuit of my academic goals, and my father lived and breathed my success.

'You can do anything, Lisa,' he'd encourage.

This was one of Dad's last comments to me. I had just received my child adolescent psychiatry advanced training certificate from the college of psychiatrists in the mail, and I'd posted a picture on my social media for everyone to see. I sensed sadness in his written words, learning of my achievement in this way. Usually, I'd first share these moments with Dad; and often, that would be enough. But feeling resentful, I punished him by withholding my news.

I'd lived to make him happy, and for many years, his beaming pride and admiration had been the lifeline of my self-worth.

Dad had had his own academic aspirations. Once he'd tried to start an accounting degree through correspondence. I would sit with him at the dining room table as he studied from what my ten-year-old eyes remember as *enormous* textbooks. Dad wasn't lazy, but for whatever reason, he never managed to finish it. He'd never addressed the many complex psychological reasons that prevented him from persisting and completing tasks (as would be the case today and forms much of the work I do). Looking back now, I think he'd lost faith in himself. It happens when one's best efforts are never met with success. I had always encouraged him as he did me, but somehow, my encouragement didn't have the power to fortify his self-belief. Self-belief and having someone believe in you builds resilience, but the direction in which these influences run perhaps rightly flow only from a parent to a child and not the other way around.

Many days I've wondered whether bolstering my clients' pursuit of greater self-worth has provided a space to heal my feelings of not being enough or failing to help my parents.

This was apparent in a session with my 14-year-old client, a few months after Dad died.

'I wish you could see in yourself what I see in you,' I said as I looked over at Mina, who sat nervously on the edge of the tan-coloured leather three-seater couch, casually dressed in her trackpants and a t-shirt bearing the slogan: KILLIN IT. *What she unconsciously hoped to be doing in her life,* I'd imagined. Most of her curly blond-brown hair was tied back with a scrunchie into a high ponytail, and her sad eyes were visible through large clear-framed glasses. I sensed her exasperation as she told me about her latest less-than-acceptable math result:

'I know my dad is disappointed in me. You know, it would be easier if he were mad at me, but seeing that look of disappointment on his face makes me want to die.'

I reiterated familiar comments that were the consistent theme over the weeks of our therapy aimed at enhancing her self-worth.

'Your math is something you do. You aren't your math. Are there objective reasons you performed badly this time around?'

Her earnest expression was a picture of thoughtfulness. I continued, 'As you know, when failure happens, it's an opportunity. Let's consider how we work through this. What do you think?'

She nodded. I felt bolstered knowing I was supporting to rebuild what she experienced as damaged or defective.

Had my dad felt damaged or defective? There had been numerous times where I had to step up financially to bail Dad out of a bad debt situation, and those times stretched as far back as my almost-adulthood, when I'd paid a lot of my own way through university because my father had simply not earned enough to have his own finances cover my tertiary education.

I didn't want to judge my father's station in life because it wasn't fair to him. He had done his best, and if that best wasn't good enough to save him, none of us could change it now. We are forced to live with his choices and ours –

and his death.

Long before Dad died, I'd made the decision to distance myself from him. It was a gradual process rather than an acute and deliberate move. I had become frustrated and realised I couldn't influence him to make the changes to improve his life.

Now, of course, the fact that our relationship wasn't at its best when he died, fills me with sadness and regret. I can recall a conversation where Dad was excitedly sharing a plan to get some money together to finance him and Mum moving to Australia. They were applying to emigrate, and I'd offered to finance one visa whilst he funded another. We were met with many disappointments in the process, and my irritation grew with every conversation we had about it. Dad rattled off his plan, and I remember how my abruptness and annoyance had humiliated him. Now I want to cry thinking about his shame and the hurt I caused him.

But I remind myself of the truth – Dad understood my frustration and how much I had given. He was ashamed of his apparent inadequacies and never meant to transfer his stress onto me. I'm convinced this is why he eventually stopped asking me directly for help. Dad would want me to have compassion for myself. I had made my choices and done what I'd needed to do, and *that* couldn't be changed now or ever.

But none of this erases my sadness when I think about how our relationship has been left so unresolved, with so much left unspoken. *Why was I the child to have this responsibility, this relationship and this unpleasant ending? Why were my siblings able to enjoy their protected relationship with Dad? Why couldn't I just be a child and have a normal dad? Why had I been given these tough choices?*

Thankfully, I know that feelings are complicated, and that's okay. But it doesn't make living with them any easier.

CHAPTER 8

Trauma on Repeat

At the funeral, I accompanied my mother into the room where my dad lay in his coffin. She desperately wanted to see his body, and I was the only person willing to go with her.

'I have to see Sam!' she cried.

The two elderly gentlemen overseeing the funeral rites tried to stop her – apparently, it wasn't allowed or customary, but Mum was not willing to take no for an answer. She had been physically apart from my dad for slightly over three months. The last she had seen him was briefly over FaceTime in some glitchy frames on a tiny phone screen whilst Dad quietly shaved and prepped himself for the working day on the morning of the day he died. That was the farewell to all their years of marriage. She had to say her goodbyes, or else, she would never have peace and rest.

Mum had buried her mother, father and baby sister. Now she had to bury her husband. She needed these visceral moments to solidify the ethereal ending to her dearest relationships. Dad had been her life partner since they were both sixteen. Their birthdays were only ten days apart. He had two brothers and one sister, and she, two sisters and one brother. Both had lost their fathers on the 23rd of October (three years apart, many years prior.) It was as if they were destined to be together. How would Mum let go of fifty-two years of companionship?

At the funeral, she looked frail, anxious and emotionally overwhelmed as she tried to attend to family and friends. Whenever she saw a familiar face, she'd simply break down and grab hold of that person tightly to stop herself from collapsing. The tiny room where the closest family huddled together in anticipation of the proceedings was stuffy with disbelief and melancholy. We were directionless, one minute standing and then sitting again, having to share four sorrowful, discoloured fabric and wooden one-seater chairs that over the years had seated countless mourners. There were no appropriate responses to soothe Mum. My heart broke for her.

Life had been cruel to her.

By the time she was twenty-seven, she was a mother of three children, all under the age of three years. She and my father had wanted to leave South Africa to create a life in America, mindful of the imminent disaster being created by the apartheid government. The political climate at the time was volatile. The year of my birth, 1976, marked the Soweto Riots that rocked the world. My father told me years later that he dreamed of making a new home somewhere else with the promise of safety for his family. Financial and emotional obstacles prevented him from making it happen (yet another one of Dad's failed plans). Instead, my parents 'semi-grated' from the city of Cape Town to a small Afrikaner country town, Worcester. There, Dad opened a fabric store while my mother took care of her babies with the help of a domestic worker.

But Mum felt like an alien in Worcester. She had no friends, spoke very poor Afrikaans and was lost without her mother, who was a rock in her life. Mum had an enmeshed and dependent relationship on my grandmother who was a strong, kind woman and protective of her family. My grandmother was a woman of valour and true belonging. She had no qualms ending a relationship with anyone who wrongfully treated her or a member of her family. I can recall countless times my mother spoke about her dependency on my grandmother and how when she moved away from her mother, she lost the self-sufficiency to cope with basic day-to-day tasks.

Then my grandmother became ill and was admitted to hospital for bypass surgery, a procedure not so simple in the '80s in South Africa. My mother recalls her mum lying in her hospital bed, mute from the tracheotomy and gesturing for a pen and paper on which to write, 'Get me Chris Barnard!' My grandmother thought that perhaps this world-renowned, pioneering South African doctor could save her life, but that was a wish no-one could grant her.

One day Mum was called to come urgently to the hospital, but the trip from Worcester to Cape Town took too long, and she never got to say her goodbyes to her mother. And just like that, she lost her anchor. I'd judged her over the years, for her weak ad nauseum perseveration about this tragic moment; but now, having lost my father, suddenly, I understood. My mother's world, as she knew it, fell to pieces and so did her capacity to care for herself, her husband and her three young children.

I was only three years old and too young to understand what was then described as a nervous breakdown, a severe anxiety and depression that wiped out her ability to cope, but the mark it left on me still aches. Like a family recipe, Mum's grief – a mixture of her anxiety, heartbreak and emptiness – was passed down. I remember seeing my mother curled up, lying in her bed, oozing sadness. It permeated the space around her and us. She had lost her mother; and at the same time, we lost ours too. The pain of her grief became a shared burden, and the baton of unresolved emotion was passed on, as is the case with intergenerational trauma.

Three months later, my grandfather was murdered on his walk home from playing cards with friends. He was only metres from his home. This gentle giant of a man was stabbed to death and bled out on the streets as no-one came to his aid. The motive: a wristwatch. After this, my mother broke into smaller pieces, and the paper-thin divide between her and us expanded to canyon-like proportions. She was still a physical presence in our lives, but emotionally and psychically, she'd become a ghost. I asked Mum only recently what we did when she was crying inconsolably, and she said that we would put our arms around her and say, 'Mum, please don't cry.'

We can now laugh about it together when I tell her that I became a psychiatrist at the ripe old age of three.

I've blocked out many memories from those early days. Humans have poor or no memory for traumatic or emotionally challenging experiences. In these moments, we flee by disassociating, overwhelmed by feelings of fear and sometimes deep shame, guilt or sadness. It is difficult to be attentive and engaged enough to lay down well-integrated memories for such events.

As a child, it hurt to see my mother's sorrow, and I feared her distress. For some reason, I felt responsible, which caused me even more pain. Disassociation was the life jacket my brain threw out to help me survive an overwhelmingly and insoluble situation – a mental escape was my only exit. I was a child, floundering in an ocean of terror, guilt and self-blame. When I went within, I could shut out my surrounds; and hopefully, I'd be invisible to my mother rather than a source of her pain. Regardless of these defences, the smudges of my negative feelings were forever imprinted into my self-view. Even more disconcerting was that 'zoning out' and disassociating engulfed all my memories, and sadly, good ones went down the drain too. I wish I had more happy moments from my past to comfort me, but complicated situations erase the positive as well as the negative.

As if she hadn't had enough trauma, my mum's youngest sister, Joan, then lost a baby at full-term. Being the eldest daughter, my mum had to support her sister. My mother remembers lying together on the hospital bed, holding the lifeless baby in her arms.

'Isn't he beautiful?' my aunt asked as they stroked his head and wept. And my mum agreed.

A twenty-four-year-old Joan fell pregnant again, and finally, it was a happy moment for all. But only for three months. All in a moment, my aunt couldn't breathe. Her husband Joe suspected an asthma attack and called an ambulance, but it was too late. Later, it was believed that she'd experienced clotting caused by the pregnancy, resulting in a pulmonary embolism. No matter the cause, my mother's sister Joan was now gone too – and with her went her unborn baby and any hope for a brighter future.

I have little conscious recollection of these moments and sadly, only snippets of loving memories of my grandparents and young aunt. Yet my subconscious stored these emotional memories for decades.

Many years later, in April 2003, on the weekend of my wedding, my cousins and I were enjoying a breakfast of salmon and bagels at a popular deli on Sea Point's Main Road.

'You know Joe Goldman works next door at the pharmacy?' my sister asked me. 'Should we go say hi?' Joe Goldman had been Joan's husband.

I remembered being five years old, mesmerised by my young aunt and uncle who were a fairy-tale couple. They had clearly adored each other, were always demonstrative in their shared affection and seemed happiest in each other's company. One of my loveliest days had been as a bridesmaid at their wedding, dressed up like a princess in a blue chiffon dress, carrying a white basket of flowers as I proudly followed Joan down the aisle, she walked sadly without either of her parents.

We loved when they babysat, as we got to stay over at their apartment. In our childhood innocence, we'd toss Joe and Joan's cigarettes over the balcony because, 'You shouldn't smoke!' Their love for us superseded punishment for our mischievous antics.

* * *

Cindy and I entered the pharmacy, eager and nervous to see Joe for the first time in over two decades. *Would he recognise us?*

My sister walked ahead. 'Hi, Joe. How are you? I'm Cindy, Denise's daughter. Lisa is here too.' Joe stood silently looking at us. I slowly walked towards him and opened my mouth to say hello, but I began to cry. Joe hugged me, and we both cried, sharing our grief from a mutual loss so many years before.

* * *

Knowing the story about my mum and the tragic way she'd lost her own parents too young was always part of my life – just another page or two in the story that made up our family. I accepted her experience without realising the ways it might have shaped the person she became, and how it informed her ability to mother her children. Most days after work and every Saturday, Mum would spend time at her closest friend's home while we stayed with Dad. As I grew older, I frequently expressed anger and disappointment at my mother and her friend. *Why hadn't Mum's friend told her to go home to her young children?* I raged at her friend's failure to protect us and at my mother's behaviour. Back then, I could not see that the reason she did so was not because she loved us less but because she needed a surrogate mother. I never intuited that her actions were involuntary and an inept response to her emptiness. I was aggressive and hateful towards her, feeling that her actions were deliberate and selfish.

Those were dark times, and I wasn't a psychiatrist then. I exhibited the typical lack of insight of a kid. Yes, we might *know* some critical part of our parents' history but we simply accept it, without ever using it as a reference point to explain their transition from the person they were before and the person they became after.

We don't have empathy because we don't *understand* yet. We don't realise the impact that life can have on a person – other than our own obsession with ourselves and how everything, no matter how insignificant, impacts *us*.

Once I'd studied and practised psychiatry and become a mother myself, I developed a different perspective on my mother. Many aspects of my childhood started to make more sense. My opinion about the type of mother she'd been had softened and expanded further after losing Dad. I could reflect on the losses she'd suffered so young while having to care for three little ones. It gave me a better understanding of her trauma and why she'd had those breakdowns and sometimes couldn't cope and be there for us. Her unresolved trauma overwhelmed her capacity to attend to our emotional needs. In losing her mother, my mum regressed to a child – and a child cannot care for another child.

A child needs a parent. And I had been playing parent to my mother since I was a child.

CHAPTER 9

A Personal Farewell

Now at my father's funeral, I stood alongside my Mother, admirable in the strength she displayed. I agreed to go into the room with her but told her, 'I'm too scared to see Dad. What if I see something that haunts me forever? Or I can't handle what I see and how I react? What if I remember Dad like this, and the image never leaves my mind? I'm sorry, Mum. I won't be able to get too close to Dad, but I will go into the room with you. I just won't look.'

Mum wanted to remove the sheet that was covering his face and look at him. I was surprised by her bravery. I honoured her wish and stayed in the room, but I didn't dare to look myself. She asked the two men who were standing watch whether she could remove her Magen David (Star of David) necklace to place on Dad's neck. Mum wanted a lasting connection to Dad, and it was her way of doing that.

'I'm sorry. We can't allow it,' the man said. He was soft-spoken and empathetic, clearly seeing her pain but constrained by the rules.

Standing in the room with Mum was bizarre. It was heartbreaking to hear her speak to Dad, as if he were alive and could hear every word. I wanted to look and not look both at the same time. I caught a glimpse of Dad's forehead. I couldn't manage anything more. *How was Mum so fearless in her love for him?*

'He's so cold,' she said, as if someone needed to do something to warm him up. 'I love you, Samuel. We all love you. The kids love you, Cindy, Lisa and Ralph, and the grandchildren.'

She bent over the coffin and placed her head close to his face and on his chest. She pulled up the sheet to warm him.

'He's so cold,' she said again.

Then she simply kissed him goodbye and thanked the two men who had allowed her to have this moment to farewell her husband, and together, we walked into the room where everyone gathered for the start of the funeral service.

'They stitched him up,' she whispered to me as her hand made the motion of the cuts that I knew sliced across his neck. 'I saw only one big cut.'

It's frustrating what you remember and what you forget. I wish Dad's funeral had been captured on video so I could completely absorb the experience by watching it again. What I do remember is that the Rabbi spoke tenderly and thoughtfully about my father and read out a beautiful letter my daughter, Daniella, had written to her grandfather. She'd called me to her bedroom the day before I left for South Africa and handed me the letter.

'Make sure you read this to Pa at his funeral,' she'd insisted. Her sadness was insurmountable. She had lost her closest ally, and it was imperative that she have her farewell. I silently read the letter, and the sadness poured from my eyes.

You're my best friend...
I'll miss you…Mr Hankins

Dad had always played school with the girls. He was always game to their imaginative play. Dad was fondly referred to as Mr Hankins, who had been a teacher at the girls' school. That was his role in their game, and they would always remember him for that.

In December 2017, I had flown Dad over from South Africa for a surprise visit so he could attend an end-of-year ballet concert in which Daniella had a solo so he could share in that moment of pride.

'Come outside. I have a surprise for you,' I'd announced to my daughters.

'Is it a dog?' Rachel had asked. They were desperate for a dog.

As soon as she saw her grandfather, Daniella had broken into tears, and Dad hugged her as she rested her head on his chest. In that moment I realised what he meant to them and how much grief Daniella held having to live in Australia without her grandparents. They had played a pivotal part in Daniella's first years as she was born and raised until she was two-and-a-half in South Africa.

Dad and Daniella had a unique bond. He was her

guiding light. Dad put so much effort into his relationships with my girls over the years, and they repaid him in love – his family was his wealth.

Everyone at the cemetery was moved by Daniella's letter. The mourners had all known my dad at some stage in their lives and were there to comfort us. I thought how pleased Dad would have been to have all these people attend his funeral. He'd always lacked self-certainty and wouldn't have anticipated this turn-out. I was quietly pleased for him.

It was an already very warm January morning in the Pine Town Cemetery in Cape Town. Following the service, the Rabbi ushered the mourners outside the hall for the funeral procession to Dad's official gravesite. Me, my mother, sister, brother, aunts and uncles stood motionless in a line on the harsh concrete paving; together, but separately processing our pain and loss. Approximately ninety-six hours had passed since first hearing about Dad's disappearance. We were all still in shock and confused by where we found ourselves.

Then the Rabbi walked down our human line of wilting shoulders and bowed heads, stopping in front of each one of us and earnestly reciting his blessing: '*Barukh atah Adonai Eloheinu melekh ha' olam dayan ha'emet*' (Blessed are You, Adonai Our God, Ruler of the Universe, the True Judge). Then he ripped open the left side of our white shirts over the chest area. We'd each chosen the cloth representations of our grief in the days prior, in anticipation of this process to wear for the remainder of the *shiva* period – morning and night for seven days – as a reminder of our loss. I'd seen this tradition performed before – today, it was my turn. The Rabbi addressed me tenderly and then he tore open my shirt. The rip felt somatic.

Judaism views death as a two-sided coin. When someone dies, the tragedy is undeniable, and the feelings of loss and distance seem impossible to mend. Sitting *shiva* for seven days with close family and friends who share your grief is an acknowledgement of the tragedy. But as a mourner, you can also be in denial, feeling that your loved one really hasn't gone. Although I am not overtly religious, I shamelessly held on to my faith tightly and gratefully as it embraced my brokenness and taped up the breaches in my understanding of why this devastation had occurred. I was comforted by the belief that Dad's soul existed before he was born and continued to exist after his death; and that his soul remained with me so that even though we were apart on the surface, we were still – deep inside – inseparable.

Dad's family and friends hoisted his coffin as if it were an honour. I stood behind the coffin and placed my palm affectionately on the cool surface of the dark wood. Stroking it gently, I leaned forward and kissed the container that embalmed my father. I whispered softly, 'Goodbye, Daddy. I love you forever.' *How fragile life is.* My mind felt cluttered as I walked slowly behind the wooden vessel. The clear blue Cape Town sky arched above us in antithesis to the blackness of this day. I kept envisioning Dad naked inside, his body draped in the white sheet. A single thought re-emerged, as if the repeat button had been activated in my brain. How futile life seemed – the hours of worry and work – reduced to nothing.

'You can't take it with you.' I had heard my mother say many times during my life, and now it made perfect sense.

At his funeral, I did not think about Dad's achievements or lack of assets but reflected on the impact he'd had on my life. I imagine everyone else was doing the same.

I didn't want to let go of his coffin, as if touching the shiny wooden surface meant I was able to still touch him. I felt so close to him in that moment – just me and him and my goodbye. My heart broke to see my father being lowered into the ground as each thud of sand that hit his coffin interrupted the stillness, signalling his removal from this world forever.

This has become a sad memory because as time passes, I feel more distant from him. I never want to forget him, and I never will. But it's also hard to stay close to someone who isn't physically present in our lives. Sometimes even the idea that I once had a father feels unreal.

A light goes out when you lose someone significant, as if some part of your life's energy dissipates. One moment you are charged with this life force; and suddenly, it's dimmed and depleted, diminishing and even obliterating our self-care, reason for living or our sense of meaning. We feel that life will never be the same again. Perhaps, because that is literally true, but even more so because we have lost a part of ourselves that we can never ever get back; and nothing else can ever take its place. We feel empty and broken to the point of physical pain. There is absolutely nothing that could ever make it right. Nothing has the power to bring back what we have lost. Grief is a process that can truly never be fully resolved.

What we have to do is learn to live with the irreplaceable loss forever.

CHAPTER 10

No Time to Grieve

'I need answers. I can't pretend everything is okay, because it isn't.' I was frustrated as I spoke to Cindy over the phone.

'You don't have to. We all grieve differently,' she said.

Instead of being able to grieve guilt-free through the period of *shiva*, the protected week of stillness and reflection for mourners supported and distracted by visiting family and friends, I couldn't just sit quietly. Frankly, the thought of it made me anxious – as it always did, perhaps due to my ADHD (Attention Deficit Hyperactivity Disorder). I couldn't be mindful, reflective and mourn Dad in a meaningful way because of the task ahead of me. Time is finite; timing is not. I wasn't ready to be in a place of stillness. I visualised putting my grief in a cupboard – I knew it was there and would have to be opened, reshuffled and neatly packed away; but now wasn't the time. I would have to mourn later. There were too many things to do and very little time to do them. Each second was precious.

'I need your help in investigating the cause of Dad's death,' I insisted. But it was clear my sister was not going to do so.

Her refusal felt like a punch in the belly.

'It's fine. I'm used to doing everything on my own!' I said with bitter condescension. I was infuriated by indifference in a cause that was consuming me and envious of family members who could grieve when I felt robbed of the opportunity. My frustration wasn't entirely their fault. My self-worth always defaulted into rescuing and fixing, and Dad's death had activated this dynamic in my psyche. These roles validated my sense of self.

I felt Mum's expectations of me to provide direction and solutions, and as always, I wanted to be the 'good girl' everyone admired. But I also needed answers to soothe my confusion.

The day after Dad's funeral, I kicked into gear. I made dozens of phone calls to the security company, forensic pathologist and Dad's work colleagues, scrutinising every tiny piece of information, determined to find out how and why Dad was killed. The burden of sorting out my family's problems was once again mine alone to shoulder, and I felt angry with Dad for laying this on me and imagined saying, 'Thanks for adding to my responsibility and my to-do list even when you are dead!'

He'd have appreciated my honesty. My father understood emotions even though he had no formal training. His ability to care and his lack of ego allowed those around him to express themselves without becoming defensive. He exuded a natural empathy. Dad's death made me question empathy and its complexity, as is the case for most human traits. Although Dad had inherent empathy, he wasn't perfect (who is) nor was he always empathetic. I pondered how we quantify a lack of empathy which is a characteristic of antisocial personality disorder, sociopaths and psychopaths, yet is speckled to varying degrees within all of us. I became intrigued about just how lacking in empathy one needs to be to take another human life. This conundrum is evidenced in the mixed research on the success of teaching empathy to criminals.

I also spoke to the last people to have seen Dad alive – my mother and Rachel over FaceTime, a neighbour and Bear. None of them had noticed anything unusual about Dad's mood or manner. But I wondered whether someone would give away their intentions to end their life in mannerisms or words.

I knew from experience that the decision to commit suicide sometimes brings a sense of relief and peace, mistaken by onlookers for 'normal,' or 'nothing out of the ordinary.' So I found no answers there.

I urgently needed to visit the place where Dad was found dead even though I'd heard Ralph, Jake and Bear talk about the ghastly bloodiness of the scene. The police had indicated that Dad had bled out copious amounts of blood in rapid time due to the aspirin he was taking acting as a blood thinner. But I wasn't satisfied with second-hand information. I would only find peace from personal deductions.

Despite my terror and antipathy, I hoped this necessary visit would provide me with clues and answers to his mystery death.

CHAPTER 11

Gut Instinct

The gates to the car yard opened slowly, and I heard the familiar crunching of gravel under the weight of car tires. I had visited at Dad's work many times over the years. It felt unreal being there again and under such nightmare-like circumstances.

We parked outside the second gate that formed the entrance to the car yard where two huts stood. As I got out of the car, I felt the sun burn my skin. Suddenly, I remembered, *Dad hated the heat.* I looked over at the wooden hut Dad had called the *hokkie*, an Afrikaans word meaning 'cell.' This was Dad's depressing prison cell where he sat day after day trying to make a living. Through the heat haze, I imagined Dad with sweat trickling down from his bald head to his bushy black eyebrows as he sat in front of his old portable electric fan that lived on his desk. Dad would set it to its highest speed as the stifling air circulated around the hut.

I struggled to walk as if I was being led to the edge of

a cliff. I thought of Ralph entering only days before, even more unprepared for what he would find. My heart raced, and my breathing became shallower and faster.

I followed my mother, Bear and Dad's long-term lawyer and friend, Keith, to the workshop that was in close proximity to the two huts. The short walk seemed longer than usual. Bear was rambling. Although I knew him as a fast talker, today he was quicker, ejecting bits of information about the whereabouts of Dad's scooter, the presence of two box cutters and a knife, his contact with Dad on that day, and how Dad was found lying in the office which was locked from the inside. My head felt scrambled with all the noise.

Jason, my partner, was with me but refused to go in, unable to face the shocking scene behind the wooden door.

Bear turned the key in the lock. It was time to step inside and face my father's final hours.

Although I have faced many terrible and traumatic scenes, having worked in some of the world's largest hospitals, servicing crime-ridden areas during my years of studying medicine in South Africa, I had never seen such gruesome, brutal chaos. It was excruciating to witness the space in which my father spent his final, panicked and desperate moments. I was stunned. I struggled to breathe and felt a rising nausea from my stomach to my throat. My body moved between fright, flight and freeze as I struggled to ingest the heinousness of the scene.

'How did this happen? Oh my god, Dad! Poor Dad! You were in so much pain. Oh my god, Dad. I'm so sorry that you had to be so hurt, and feel so panicked and afraid.' I sobbed as I walked around as if in circles, looking everywhere but not taking in much detail. The prospect of Dad's last moments pained me. I still feel as if I am lost for words to articulate exactly what I saw that day. It was stomach-churning to digest that it was my father's blood smeared on the walls, toilet, basin, sink, floors and furniture. Most shocking to conceive was that he had apparently been tortured.

Confronted with the unimaginable, my mind detached. This is a mechanism that kicks in to protect us in moments of shock. My memories of that day are a patchwork of separate and disseminated images in my brain. What remains are scattered and jaded details of the room.

On the floor lay scattered blood-ridden, scrunched pieces of newspapers. Suddenly, I recognised Dad's blue-checked shirt, ripped and blood-soaked, obviously torn from his body. *That was one of Dad's favourites.* I was astonished to discover that the police had left it behind, following their cursory two-hour investigation of the premises after Ralph, Jake and Bear found Dad and called them. *Why was such valuable evidence left behind on the scene?* The day Dad died, I also later ascertained, the police had handed Ralph Dad's blood-stained keys that had been lying on the office desk. They had only taken Dad's body, a pair of old worn shoes and the weapons – two box cutters and a knife.

At first, the police had declared it a murder scene but soon deemed it a suicide because there was no evidence of a break-in; only Dad's footprints were evident, and the office door had been locked. They didn't fingerprint the area or question witnesses. Only two DNA samples were taken. I wondered whether I would have been more insistent with the police than Ralph had been. Would I have pushed back, questioned and refused to give up until they completed a more thorough investigation? The truth is I don't know how my ability to act decisively would have been impacted if I'd been the one who'd found Dad. My brother did the best he could at the time.

As I entered that room where Dad had died, I felt with unwavering certainty that my father had been killed. It was *my* truth, and it emerged from deep within my core, my gut – and I trusted it.

I walked around, furious and not shy to yell out, 'He was murdered. Someone here has to know more!' I hoped Bear, who'd been intimately involved in Dad's business affairs, would let me in on what he knew. I was sure there was more than he was giving away. I was aggressive, and it made Bear jumpy at first, but he later pushed back against my insinuations that he had more information. All I could gather was that Dad had run into financial problems and was scrambling for a solution until business improved again. It seemed that he knew he was in danger. He needed more time to sort things out, but time had run out.

I filmed every corner of the room on my iPhone, hoping that I might find an incriminating piece of evidence.

It was creepy to be standing in the last place Dad had been alive only days before.

But in that terrible place, I had a sense of his soul; and in a strange and sad way, it made me feel closer to him.

CHAPTER 12

Choosing Between Forgiveness or Acceptance

'Had you given your Dad the money he owed me, he would still be alive today,' Elon's words wounded me. He was my dad's main creditor, now claiming that my dad intended to shirk his financial obligations.

'What do you mean?' my voice shook.

'Lisa, your father lied to me. I was so disappointed in him.'

I could understand his exasperation. I had also been frustrated with my father, but Elon's coldness took me by surprise. They'd been friends. *Surely, that counted for something? Perhaps there was more I didn't know.*

I had called Elon three times to try and gather as much information as possible. I insinuated foul play and suggested to him that Dad had been murdered. I wanted to know the truth. From our previous calls, I'd been able to deduce that Dad had angered people by not honouring his debts timeously. Dad's actions had appeared dubious.

Though I never questioned my father's intentions or inherent honesty, I could understand why others had begun to doubt him.

My grief was hijacked by these considerations. I struggled to be objective. I wanted desperately to protect my father while simultaneously manage my shame at how he'd behaved. Over the years, I'd internalised a sense of responsibility to my family where I constantly had to help out or be littered by reactive guilt.

As I began to clearly understand the extent of Dad's despair, I started to wonder whether he had, in fact, been driven to take his own life. Hopelessness is a trigger for suicide. As is isolation – and seeing as though none of us were aware of Dad's strife, because he had chosen not to tell us, he had suffered alone. Perhaps Dad had been like a fearful animal, trapped in a cage without any escape.

'I kind of get it,' Ralph said to me one day, long after Dad had passed away. 'I know how it feels to have no money and to be panicked about how you're going to make ends meet and repay people you owe money to. You think about killing yourself.'

As the provider of my family, I related to the sense of responsibility and feelings of uselessness when you can't meet your obligations to the people you care about the most.

I could hear the desperation in Ralph's tone. He too knew that fear.

Over the years, I've treated many clients who grew up in homes where money and education were as absent as their caregivers – and the kitchen table was scattered with beer bottles and cigarette ashes rather than eggs and toast. The weight of transgenerational trauma, abuse and neglect drags people down, even those of us who are adamant to survive and thrive.

Our early life circumstances create what we come to know as the familiar. Without using it as a scapegoat for failure, it clearly impacts on the trajectory of our lives. It is easier to succeed if we have role models of success or we are given sufficient means. Of course, it's possible to still succeed without them, but it requires a lot more work and determination.

Money sustains our livelihood, but greater wealth extends our options in life. I don't believe it buys happiness, but without money, people can become desperate and make poor choices. For me, money has always represented safety and independence rather than luxury and power.

'I think the right thing for you to do, Lisa, would be to pay me the money your dad owed me,' Elon concluded. This left me completely flummoxed.

Was it my obligation to settle Dad's debts and restore his honour? Maybe. If I didn't, would his name be besmirched forever? Would people think badly of him? I didn't want that.

It was a horrible, familiar agony, being tangled in Dad's muddied business affairs; and I was struggling to understand my ethical responsibility. I was in a three-way game of tug-of-war between my anger at Dad at not being able to repay his debts; my guilt for feeling this way; and trying to work out if making things right was, in fact, my problem.

My critical super-ego and inner moral compass

suggested I should repay the money. Then I was jolted into monstrous notions that perhaps Dad's life was a fair payback for a massive debt. I was instantly shocked by my own thoughts. What was wrong with me? How could anything justify a murder? Had I no empathy?

It was an impossible situation. Thinking in simple black-and-white terms was my way of gaining comfort with my decisions. I agonised over whether Dad was right or wrong – would that clarity help direct my actions?

The torturous childhood shame surrounding my family was like a stubborn mole that insisted on peeping out of its dark hole. Worse was that my father's dealings were now exposed in the public domain, a blemish for all to see and judge; and it hurt knowing how negatively people viewed him. *That's my father you're talking about.*

I knew I had to tolerate my discomfort to support my imperfect father who, I had to reluctantly concede, had made some terrible mistakes and choices in his life. I had to use all my training as a psychiatrist to expand and make room for all my emotions which were all reasonable and valid. I couldn't succumb to binary thinking. It didn't matter what was right or wrong. It is never that simple. I had to hold every conflicting emotion and give myself time to reflect, digest and accept.

To forgive someone is difficult. Sometimes the hurt is too great and we simply can't forgive. When we forgive, we set a precedence of tolerance, which may enable the forgiven person to continue to transgress our boundaries. In the process, we collude in their continued powerlessness, lack of responsibility and inability to own their own behaviour.

Dad always gave everyone second chances, so he likely would have expected the same from others.

In the midst of my grief, I was infuriated with Dad as I had been many times. I wished he had been a more capable businessman. Once again, I'd been left to fix the mess. But this time, I knew what I had to do.

I had to stand up. I had to insist on good boundaries. I told Elon, 'I will not repay my father's debts. I don't condone my father's actions, and I am sorry that you have been negatively affected. I know my dad didn't mean to hurt anyone, but unfortunately, he did. But I am not responsible for that.'

I could no longer blame my past. I could make my choice, and I did.

But I was haunted by the question: was my father a bad person?

He'd always been generous to his staff and co-workers, providing soup in winter for his watchman to keep warm, helping others with rent and monthly bills, and always ensuring Christmas time was special with food, bonuses and toys for his workers' children.

It was a blessing then, after Dad died, to receive a call from a stranger, who introduced himself as one of Dad's old school friends.

'Your father was a gentleman. He'd always come and have a coffee with me when he came to Paarl for business. I had a stroke a few years back, and your dad always called me to check if I was okay. He always made the time to talk and showed such an interest.'

As he spoke, I cried.

His love and respect for my father reinforced what I

knew – my dad had always been a forgiving and tolerant man. Those are the values he raised us with. Who was I to judge the way life's challenges had stripped him of options so that he ended up making mistakes, misjudgements and misdemeanours? Dad's errors were an inexorable part of his human nature. Now by societal rules and standards, he was being judged negatively. Where did love belong in this context? What about forgiveness for the sin of being human after all?

I battled to know how to feel.

With time, I have come to understand that sometimes we struggle to forgive someone when the damage they have left in their wake is too great. Perhaps forgiveness is not the goal then. Or perhaps something else precedes it – acceptance. No matter what feelings are evoked, we can always accept what has happened. Acceptance doesn't excuse the wrong. When we accept what has happened, we acknowledge the devastation, disappointment and pain, especially when the person who has hurt us is meant to love and care for us. It allows and tolerates all feelings without judgement. When we accept, we exercise the self-compassion that allows us to move forward.

In the weeks and months that followed, I had to find a way to accept Dad and the torturous truth of the dire circumstances that led to his death – whether it was murder or suicide.

CHAPTER 13

Questioning Reality

'Lisa, you won't believe it, but I found Dr Forpath's book in Dad's desk.' Cindy was calling me from Dad's office two days after I'd been there. Mum was with her as well as a forensic expert we'd engaged.

Eric Forpath, an esteemed forensic expert, had been recommended to my Uncle David to help us unravel the mystery surrounding Dad's death. In the irrationality of my shock, I had impulsively paid him a generous sum of money to visit Dad's death scene and provide his opinion. I had hoped for miracles, which precluded me thinking through all the possible outcomes of enlisting his services.

What was Dr Forpath's book doing in Dad's desk? The coincidence was eerily spooky.

Dad had enjoyed reading and was often immersed in a mystery or crime novel. But this was my aunt's book. The letters of her name, *Diana Myers*, were written in blue ink on the inside cover. 'Dad must have borrowed it from Aunty Diana?' It was both a statement and a question.

'What? We cleared everything out Dad's office two days ago!' My mind boggled. I began to distrust my previous clarity. 'I'm sure we emptied his desk.' I was almost certain that book had not been there forty-eight hours ago.

'And you won't believe this, but Dad's bookmark was in the chapter describing South African mining magnate, Brett Kebble's orchestration of his own murder,' Cindy continued.

'Do you think it's possible Dad staged his death? But why would he want to be tortured? Dad owned a gun. Why not use that? It doesn't make any sense – nothing does. Who do we trust? I don't know what to think or believe anymore!'

A thick black fog of uncertainty descended. I felt a wedge burrowing between me and the man I had known as my father.

Dr Forpath's book in my dad's desk brought up new questions, unsettling my grief and loss once again. A few days before, I had stood with utter conviction in that room, trusting my instinct that Dad had been brutally murdered. Now I couldn't trust my gut, anything or anyone. It was unnerving to discover all these disturbing facts about someone I believed I knew so well. I felt as if I was on *The Truman Show*, foolishly blind to what those around me could see while I remained oblivious.

Let me decode what happens psychologically when we make an unexpected finding. We question our past judgement. We become confused and distrust our perceived reality. If we discover an affair in an apparent loving relationship, drug abuse or porn addiction in a well-mannered child, or sexual abuse in the family, our trust is shattered, causing conflicted emotions, disconnected thoughts and a loss of clarity on what is real. We struggle to be decisive and sink deeply into the quicksand of confusion and fear as we question everything we once believed to be true. We become increasingly sceptical of any new information. Depending on the circumstances, once shock settles, we might feel ashamed, foolish and the need to hide. We become paranoid that every innocent glance is a negative judgement or that there is danger everywhere. Finally, we may feel pain as we grieve the loss of the person or relationship we knew.

Traumatic revelations create mental confusion. If we don't continually process and integrate these troubling experiences, we remain emotionally and psychologically unsettled. We can easily be retriggered, sometimes by the slightest occurrence or another traumatic incident. In a flash, we are transported from the present moment back to the initial terror where nothing makes sense. It is a terrifying experience.

As each of us acquires knowledge through our life events, we begin to construct a database of norms. Then when dots don't connect, we question that deviation from our known truth. As a doctor, I'm trained to seek patterns, like the group of symptoms that make up a diagnosis, which align with my formulated hypothesis. When I come across outliers who don't fit the pattern, I become suspicious, question my prior assumptions and the client's credibility as I consider whether there might be conscious – or unconscious – motives for them to be manipulative.

.In the light of Dr Forpath's book which felt like a new

twist, I began to ruminate about Dad's involvement in his death. It caused a massive disruption in the database of norms I used to navigate my life. I just wanted control over the uncertainty. I became more and more conflicted. I didn't know what to think anymore. I simply wanted an end to the incessant draining barrage of unanswerable questions.

Cindy relayed that after he'd surveyed the crime scene, Dr Forpath, drawing on his knowledge of patterns, formed the opinion (much like the police) that Dad had committed suicide. He based this on the lack of proof to support a break-in and that the only visible footprints belonged to Dad. Hearing Dr Forpath's verdict, I collapsed into a heap. He was my last and only hope of being able to challenge the police.

During the days that followed, Cindy and I reviewed Dad's recent internet searches, exploring whether he'd researched suicide, but all we found were questions about four and five letter words for his crosswords.

Suddenly, everything I had ever known about my father was under attack. While the rest of my family deferred to Dr Forpath's verdict, I did the unimaginable and questioned the forensic expert. As you can imagine, it didn't go down well.

I pummelled Dr Forpath with my questions as if he was a hostile witness. I dismissed everything he said because it wasn't what I wanted to hear.

'What if the perpetrator had keys, then they wouldn't have had to break in? Did you speak to the pathologist who said Dad had a few blows to his body, cuts that weren't vital, because he was likely dead when they were made and symmetrical bruising that appeared to be caused by being held down? I wrote everything in the notes I sent through to you – did you read them?'

'I don't ever read documents prior to visiting a scene. It's not essential,' he replied.

'What? That's simply insane! Dr Forpath, I have done a lot of forensic psychiatry, and the first thing I do is read all the documents prior to taking the next step.'

In my grief, I became hypercritical and frustrated with his conclusions that I felt overlooked all the angles and evidence available.

I was defensive – not only of my father but of myself as I also felt judged. I was being treated as if I was naïve. It seemed as if my family were discounting my knowledge, training, expertise and instincts. *Who did I think I was? I was not the expert; I was the grieving daughter. There was no concrete evidence to support my beliefs.* So I was dismissed. Their doubts began to infect me, and my certainty mutated to bewilderment as I began to question what my soft-spoken father was capable of and whether I was so out of touch that I couldn't conceive of what had perhaps really taken place.

Seeking closure when it doesn't exist can be torturous. I suffered for months as thoughts ran laps in my head until I realised it was all pointless. I would never know how Dad had died. Losing him was only the tip of the iceberg – I still had to process my feelings that formed a dark thick layer below the facts of his horrible death.

CHAPTER 14

Efforts in Vain

Days later, I boarded the plane back to Sydney, fragmented, trepidatious and irritated that I had to leave behind an unresolved mess. Time had run out, and I had to resume my life in Sydney.

My few days in South Africa had been an unsuccessful battle to find information, and I left more confused than when I'd arrived.

I had only given myself a week off work, naively imagining I'd attend Dad's funeral, fly back to Sydney and immediately return to work. I considered it another obligation in my already overcommitted life.

To understand my actions, you need to know that my deepest fears, having grown up without financial security, is being left completely destitute. *If I'm away from work for too long, will I return to a heap of rubble? I will be fine if I keep control over my schedule.* So I did what I always do – I disconnected and 'just did.' I rationalised that I couldn't possibly extend my trip to further investigate Dad's death even if for only another week.

Of course, on my return to Sydney, I realised how incapable I was of working while containing my emotions and being present for my clients. Despite being consumed with grief, I tried to push through, afraid of the monetary consequences of not working and letting my clients down.

My partner Jason generously offered financial assistance which gave me permission to take care of myself.

'I will give you the money you need for the next two weeks. You cannot work.' I was so relieved and grateful to him.

For many months afterwards, I viewed my decision to return from South Africa early as selfish; but as my understanding of the impact of trauma and loss grew, I was able to forgive myself, acknowledging how harsh, unfair and unnecessary my self-judgement was. Shock is a cocktail of numbness, nothingness and at the same time, it's an overfull, scattered mess of confusing, frightening thoughts and emotions. People lose sense of time, and this is exactly what happened to me.

Self-compassion became a vital part of healing from the loss of my father. What has remained is the sadness of not taking the additional week to imbibe the experience of loss. What had felt like too long at the time was now simply a snippet dissolved into the span that made up my life.

I have made peace with the fact that we honoured Dad by not persisting with the investigations, which is likely what he would have wanted.

But we now have to live with the lack of closure, and

I will always have to sit with my frustrating regret that I didn't permit myself the time to do more and care for my needs.

Over the next six months, I continued to replay the video footage of the room in the hope that I would finally see a critical piece of evidence I'd previously missed. I obsessively envisioned the scenarios that might have played out on that day, often finding myself completely distracted by the chaos in my head.

A few months following Dad's death, the police emailed through the dossier containing all the photographs of my dad – the scene on the day, his exposed body, the autopsy photographs, witness statements, lab reports and a few other bits and pieces.

I wept as I looked at my father's naked and mutilated body. For what felt like an hour, I sat motionless in front of the laptop screen as I tried to absorb the images. I recognised his body, face, hands, arms, fingers and wrinkles – all the familiar parts of Dad. I was weirdly comforted by these photos that captured him in his final moments. I stroked the screen in front of me, gently moving over Dad's face and body, and I cried. I wanted to feel close to him and heal his pain. It was part of my goodbye and the farewell I never had.

'I love you, Dad,' I said it many times over. 'I will always love you, Dad. I am so sorry for you. How did they hurt you like this? How did we not know? Why didn't you tell me? I would have helped you.'

I envisioned being Dad's guardian angel in his moment of suffering, shielding him with my love.

What was happening is typical of how we cope in

unmanageable situations – we resort to magical thinking to experience some sense of control. It was my psyche's way of defending against my helplessness which had doggedly driven me to investigate Dad's death. I hadn't been there to help Dad in his time of need, so that had been my only way to feel useful.

I opted not to share these images with my family (although, unfortunately, my sister saw them years later). My mother pleaded to see them, but I refused. After losing my father, my mother's mind and residual coping ability became even more fragile. I was sure exposure to these images would only overwhelm and retraumatise her. The shock of Dad's death alone had caused her to develop severe PTSD. For months, she had nightmares, and she screamed and yelled profanities through the night at Dad's killers. I watched her battle to come to terms with Dad's pain and navigate her guilt for having not been with him in South Africa when it happened. Those pictures would only have exacerbated her fantasies of Dad's suffering and unnecessarily tormented her. I chose to protect my family by absorbing the trauma on my own.

But I did show the photos to a few colleagues and other professionals. I wanted their objective and unbiased opinions, but secretly, I wanted confirmation that Dad had been murdered rather than taken his own life. Truthfully, I didn't know which cause of death I found less shameful. Most of them weren't able to stomach the gruesome images.

'How do you look at your father like that, Lisa?' some asked.

In a weird way, their acknowledgement of Dad's

suffering justified my mission. The endless hours I had spent investigating Dad's death often left me questioning everything – from the facts of the case to my motives and need for answers.

Throughout this time, I was powerfully defended with my armoury of denial, suppression, rationalisation and intellectualisation. I remained determined to do something for Dad, even if it was beyond the grave. I know now that my clinical training allowed me to adopt an analytical, distanced approach which safeguarded me from the true impact of seeing the horror these images depicted.

We all have our Pandora's box of emotions filled with years of hurt, loss, rejection and suffering which we keep tightly shut for fear it will explode, leaving the mess of subconscious, unwelcome feeling-scraps scattered everywhere.

I knew that if I allowed any pain or anxiety to leak, it would engulf and crush me, leaving me fuzzy and functionless. I tightened the locks and shut out my emotional connection to Dad. I've often considered the growing distance between us that preceded his death as ironically preparatory.

It was impossibly discouraging trying to conduct investigations from the other side of the world. The South African judicial system didn't facilitate or support my efforts in any way. I was David and it was Goliath, and I lacked the resources to build a substantial case to challenge the bureaucracy.

I recognise that the South African law enforcement structures were overwhelmed with exponential crime rates and insufficient resources. I'd been through the

South African system. I understood it and at times, empathised with it. I have worked in overfull emergency departments in disadvantaged townships and have faced the overwhelming helplessness of having one hundred pairs of desperate eyes looking to me for help. Initially, you have the best intentions and try everything possible to help; but soon, the lack of support leaves you exhausted in a bottomless pit of desperate people. Everyone caught in that system becomes stretched and burnt out. It breeds despondency and a culture of complacency. Users suffer the impact.

I had been living away from South Africa for a long time and was no longer desensitised to crime (which happens when you are frequently faced with it). As an Australian citizen, I'd grown accustomed to a degree of accountability and the extensive investigations, preparation and presentation of reports to the coroner following a violent death.

Whether he'd been murdered or died by his own hand, I wanted similar action to be taken for my father. I viewed murder mysteries on television and felt frustrated, witnessing them conduct very detailed investigations. I'd return to my case notes, hopeful that I could find solutions by applying what I'd seen or heard from other cases.

I planned to present my case to the local magistrate in South Africa in June 2019, six months after Dad's death. Despite knowing it was a courtesy meeting and that he would have made his decision prior to our meeting based on the police documents, I needed to be heard. Dad's death wasn't a statistic for the census, or simply another file amongst the untold pillars of manila folders cluttering his desk. I would be the advocate for my family. I would be Dad's voice, and in doing so, I would be speaking for every person who had suffered injustice at the hands of a system that overlooked their individual suffering.

I spent months constructing a reasonable account of the events based on the available information, photos, autopsy report and expert opinions. I proposed that Dad had been taken into the office, where he had been butchered and tortured to his death. The circling of bloody footprints depicted his slow and stressed suffering that was impossible to believe was self-inflicted. My investigations had uncovered Dad's hardships and his hustling to make a living. It was painful to realise how little I'd known. I felt guilty, negligent and completely self-absorbed. Slowly, I became more fatigued and hopeless. I so badly needed this process to run its course. It seemed as if it was my destined journey to achieve the only closure I could hope for.

'Let it go.' Those close to me kept urging as they witnessed my fatigue from all the heavy lifting. 'Your Dad would understand.'

But I couldn't. I kept examining and re-examining the evidence and preparing arguments.

While all this was happening, I was neglecting to process my grief – but I wasn't ready yet. So I focused on fixing what I believed I'd broken. It's only with the clarity of hindsight and time that I've come to realise I couldn't have interjected in Dad's untimely fate or changed a thing.

CHAPTER 15

Living with Unanswered Questions

'What do you mean a letter, Ralph? You found what in your car? Send it to me immediately.'

A month after Dad's funeral, Ralph called and was audibly upset. It was late in Sydney, and I was in bed, ready to sleep. He explained that he'd discovered a black leather folder under the passenger seat of his car, and in it was a letter – written by Dad.

My heart beat like a drum as I waited for the image to land in my WhatsApp. Half-thoughts raced on a rat's wheel of panic, wondering what my brother had found. Was this a suicide note that Ralph had discovered, once again, all alone? Was I about to read it?

Ralph had been using Mum's car because she had come to Australia and had been staying with me since October 2018 for the three months before Dad's death.

'When would Dad have put the letter in Mum's car? When did you last see Dad in person?' I asked Ralph as I tried to make sense of the timing of events.

'I hadn't seen Dad since the last weekend in November. I don't know how this got in my car and why I didn't find it before.' I could hear Ralph blaming himself.

'Ralph, don't beat yourself up. This is not your fault. It makes no sense that Dad would put a suicide note in Mum's car months before killing himself. Dad would never have wanted *you* to find it. He wouldn't have put that burden on you – Dad loved you.' My body ached, registering his pain.

I wasn't sure how I'd cope, reading the suicide note of someone I so dearly loved. My anticipation was monstrous. I feared uncovering a piece of information I had potentially overlooked, didn't know, was responsible for or could have prevented.

Dad was a man of few words, and the note was no different. It was a mixture of intense fear and practicality.

His note was addressed to Mum. His urgency was obvious from his writing. It was rushed, and specific parts were underlined. His tone was stressed and direct.

'Sell everything and go to Australia. Ask Lisa to change the ticket. I will not survive in this business. I am sorry, but I have got myself into too much trouble. Lisa will take care of you…' And then he made a stupid joke: *'at least I won't need the hip replacements… Ha ha.'*

Ha ha?

At the bottom of the note, Dad had notarised all the vehicles that were on his yard at the time and the respective owners of those held on consignment so that Mum would know the rightful owner of each vehicle.

I called one of the owners whose name I recognised and determined the approximate time Dad had written the letter. It dated back to September – this was even more illogical. What was becoming clear was that my father had pre-empted his plan or his fate.

To this day, I still don't understand Dad's letter, the timing, tone and conflicting messages contained in it. Dad seemed terrified of the consequences related to the unfathomable bungle he'd found himself in, but woven through his words was a tinge of desperation, quasi farewells to family and intonations of a plan to take his life as his only remaining solution.

The note only furthered my confusion and the agonising lack of closure oxygenating my insanity. It was the snake that took me back to square one of the snakes-and-ladders board of undulating, never-ending grief.

I'd heard about the profile of those who write suicide notes and reasons people leave them. 'I wish they'd left a note,' some say. While others are distraught at discovering their loved one's final thoughts and are forever unable to remedy the hurt expressed by the deceased. Sometimes, the closure it can provide in offering insights or reasons can be offset by additional questions, creating further confusion.

From a clinical perspective, these notes help us understand suicide and can lead to preventative strategies and support for survivors. Victims frequently express guilt for their actions, likely depicting their underlying depression because overt self-blame is a common symptom of melancholy. Notes are often written shortly before the suicide, and frequently, the victims are found to be devoid of an extensive documented mental health history. I wondered whether the latter described Dad who never appeared to have any mental health problems. Dad's note was hasty but was oddly written months before his death. It was a firing of instructions, an outline of his troubles and speckled words of apology.

I questioned why Dad wouldn't have taken the time to say goodbye to any of us. I was angry that he hadn't considered how important his feedback was on how I was living life and whether I'd been a good daughter and parent. Why didn't he know how much I'd need his guidance on raising my children? I felt incensed by his selfishness and in parallel, guilty that I'd not communicated with him frequently enough and was therefore disconnected from his plight. I battled to understand that he'd needed me but had chosen to remain silent. The hardest realisation of all was that my wish for a second chance would remain empty forever – like my heart – without Dad's presence to fill it.

I reflected on his words to Mum – that I'd care for her. Dad had simply assumed, as had been the case for years, that I would take care of everything. Part of me felt honoured that he knew I would do so as I'd sacrificed so much to counteract my feelings of not being enough. But I was disappointed that Dad had not been able to discuss his troubles with me as I'd always believed we'd had a confiding relationship.

The detective assigned to his case in South Africa repeatedly questioned Dad's mental health, pushing for an admission that my father's despair had caused him to overdose on his medication, thus providing a motive. He refused to accept that Dad had never suffered from depression and wasn't prescribed psychotropic medications. I kept reiterating that Dad's only medical condition had been hypertension, and for this, he'd used aspirin and amlodipine.

Months later, I received a toxicology report, dated *before* the text from the investigating officer suggesting that further drug tests be done to determine the cause of death, despite them citing blood loss as the cause. Bizarrely, none of Dad's regular medications were found in his system, despite the initial claims that the aspirin had caused Dad's rapid bleeding and subsequent death. This was another strange finding. Instead, the report listed numerous other medications – all of which, I was familiar with as a psychiatrist: Largactil (an antipsychotic), Codeine, Tramadol (opiates), Cipramil (an antidepressant), Panadol (an analgesic) and Amlodipine (an antihypertensive). I don't know why, but intuitively, I knew the report was nothing but a duplicate from a 'typical' psychiatric patient who had overdosed. I'd seen plenty of these types of reports before. They were not typical of a sixty-eight-year-old grandfather without a mental health history. I examined and re-examined the report, and knew I'd found its falsity when I picked up an error – a discrepancy between the number on the test tube and that of the lab report.

I tried to draw the investigator and magistrate's attention to these inconsistencies, but they refused to listen. Although their theories were medically implausible, I was met with indifference and denial. I pleaded with them to explain how they married up a lethal overdose of antihypertensives with no evidence of tablets in Dad's body and the ability for him to cut himself and bleed out hours later. Only the pathologist supported my views, but this wasn't enough for us to uncover the truth. Eventually, utterly defeated, I realised I was going to have to live with their verdict.

It is a tragic coincidence that in each of the two years around the anniversary of Dad's death in December, I've lost one of my young clients to suicide (How cruel is the universe?). On both agonizing occasions, when I met with the family, my grief had been retriggered, compounding the heartache for my clients with whom I had close relationships. I was short of words to adequately comfort the parents and siblings in the swarm of pain, loss and guilt. Justifiably, they had many questions, as we all did, in our search for answers. I felt helpless, able to offer nothing more than empathy. Losing a child is unbearable and a suicide only that much more heartbreaking, complicated by the many unknowns and the lack of closure.

I never imagined a family suicide would form part of my resume. Despite the uncertainties around Dad's death, my firsthand experience made me more compassionate to the parents of my clients.

A suicide in a family evokes anger, guilt, sadness, confusion and shame.

My shame is that Dad has been judged as weak and defective. Yet, if we think about it from the sufferer's point of view, it takes immense courage to go through with suicide. A person has to overcome the enormity of fear and face the unknown abyss that follows those final moments (perhaps this further reflects the sufferer's extent of inner turmoil). I have wrestled with thoughts of Dad's last mortal minutes. I've spent agonising hours weeping as I tried to imagine his fear, pain, dread, sadness and guilt. But mostly, I refuse to let my mind go there. I don't want to envision my father's suffering.

As with so many mourners, the unanswered questions remain my greatest torment. When we don't understand why or how, we stew, grapple and deliberate, juggling our conflicting feelings that cannot – and never will be – resolved. For me, my mother and siblings, it has been challenging to accept the extremes of Dad's anguish and that he might have abandoned us.

Dad used to complain to Mum that I never called him often enough, and he missed hearing my voice. During my grief, I've yelled out, 'You complained that I didn't call you, but you couldn't even bother with a final call. Why didn't you tell me what you wanted from me, or what you thought of me. And what about your grandchildren, did they not matter to you?'

I am not sure what is easier to stomach – suicide or murder? Both are devastating and involve suffering and pain. Both provoke guilt and shame. If he did indeed take his own life, he also took my peace of mind. Dad left me nothing to make sense of his death.

In therapy, I have come to realise that Dad chose not to share his problems, and I can only imagine that was his way of safeguarding us and the little pride he had left too.

Sometimes, with the best intentions, the people we care about make choices that impact us. They act out of love and the need to protect us. I've come to a place where I can empathise with and finally respect Dad's decision. Maybe he wasn't fully present or in control, or perhaps he didn't have the time and opportunity to share the truth with us.

I am frustrated *he* got to decide that I could not handle the truth. I wonder whether it would have been easier to grieve his death if I'd had all the facts so I could process my feelings in my own way. I will never know.

Ironically, I *am* forced to manage my feelings – simply different ones.

CHAPTER 16

Time to Say Goodbye

I sat silently in the car, feeling empty and tired. The drive from Worcester to Cape Town had seemed longer than usual.

It had been a series of difficult days. It was six months since Dad's death, and I'd travelled over sixteen hours from Sydney to Cape Town with prepared notes. I'd practiced my argument and finally had my chance to face the magistrate.

'Did you see the photos? Did you see those horrible images?' I asked him.

'I did.' The magistrate replied, stone-like as he sat behind his massive desk, piled high with papers and folders. His tone was cold, dismissive and unempathetic. It was obvious that I was an inconvenience to him.

'They were awful. I had a quick look.'

I had composed myself for the initial fifteen minutes as I confidently presented my case and reasons to disprove his suicide verdict. All throughout, the magistrate was staring back at me blankly. Finally, I succumbed to my mounting emotions and cried. My brother, Ralph, sitting quietly next to me, gently placed a hand on mine.

'Well, can you imagine how this has been for me? You looked at those photos and found it horrible, and to you, it is just another person, a number. But to me, it is my father, my flesh and blood, the man who raised me. How do you think I should feel about this? How would you feel looking at your family member, and what would you want to happen? I have spent months on this, trying to find some kind of justice and to have answers to this heinous crime. I have flown halfway across the world to have this moment, to get someone to help my family get some peace.'

I could hardly get the words out. I was shaking so much as the tears ran down my face.

The magistrate looked at me impassively. 'I have no medical knowledge. I am satisfied with what it is in this file. This has taken enough time now. Thanks for coming. Have a nice day.'

That was it. The hearing was over, investigations completed and cause of death concluded. My heart sank. I felt numb and lifeless. I was powerless, unable to speak or move.

Right then, I heard Dad's voice inside me, urging me to let go and continue with my life. I knew he would have been proud of my efforts.

It was time for me to move on.

* * *

Before I'd left for South Africa, I'd told Mum that I'd done my best to find out what had happened to Dad and would do the same in trying to convince the magistrate.

'This is my last chance. I am not hopeful, but I will give it my all – as I always do and have done so far,' I'd said.

Mum naively believed I would find Dad's killers.

'Once I leave South Africa, no matter the outcome, I am moving forward with my life. I suggest you do too. We can't keep going around in circles, wondering what happened to Dad. It's irrelevant. Dad is gone, and nothing will bring him back,' I'd said.

After the magistrate's verdict, I had to honour my commitment to myself to finally let it all go.

Returning to Cape Town, we stopped at the cemetery to visit Dad's gravesite. This would be my time to say my last goodbye. I left Ralph at the car, needing time alone with Dad.

I walked slowly with my head bowed towards Dad's grave. The air was cool and the cemetery quiet. The old brick pathways were familiar. I sat down cross-legged in front of his grave, only a mound of sand with a small peg board in the ground alongside it bearing his name, 'Myers, Samuel.' Sitting on the hard brick pathway, I let the sand that covered his grave gently run through my fingers, soothing me just as I'd done as a child with the satin edge of my yellow blanket.

After a few moments, I spoke to Dad.

'I'm sorry, Daddy,' I whispered through my tears as I sat with my heart open and tender in front of him. 'I'm sorry I couldn't solve your death. I'm sorry this happened.'

My tears formed a solid dark blob in the wet sand.

Table Mountain loomed large in the distance. Everything around me was quietly motionless, and as I looked at the surrounding grave sites, I thought about the untold pain represented by many lost loved ones. I was surrounded by the sands and stones of grief. Despite my heartache, I was at peace, close to my father. It was surreal to remember his burial only months before and to imagine his decomposed remains in a coffin below me.

I did not want these closing moments with Dad to end.

'I love you forever. Thank you for being the best Dad I could have hoped for. I am sorry I was so hard on you. I know you were only trying your best. I will care for Mommy, I promise.'

I sat silently for what seemed long, but too short. I cried and cried, then wiped my tears, stood up and walked away, not looking back.

PART 2

Our Stories

In all moments of darkness,
we can find the light of meaning.

CHAPTER 17

Making Mental Space for Others

I was extremely anxious about returning to work, knowing I was responsible for the care of many vulnerable people. I felt fragile and doubted my usual ability to contain my clients' emotions, given how much I was struggling to hold my own feelings together.

What I found was that many of my clients were conflicted when they saw me again, as if they felt guilty for burdening me with their 'minor' issues, even as they were desperate for the support, they'd come to receive from me. I did my best to ease their reservations.

'You can't compare, and you don't need to. I'm thankful that you can acknowledge my hurt; and I know you feel responsible for fixing it and don't feel comfortable sharing your struggles with me, but it's not needed. That is not appropriate now. Perhaps we can think together why you are feeling so triggered by this.' I'd say, trying to reassure them.

But my emotional unavailability reignited many of my

clients' past difficulties with attachment, increasing their abandonment anxiety and rejection sensitivity. I became their 'preoccupied mother' consumed by trauma, as mine had been years before, after her losses. I knew it was critical to compartmentalise my grief and limit the overspill of emotions into the therapy relationship in order to hold the anxious, angry inner child within the unsettled adult sitting across from me.

I can remember, as a little girl, seeing my mother sitting on the edge of the old, reupholstered couch that had been her mother's. She had always clung desperately to anything and everything that kept her connected to her parents. She'd sit curled over, like an erect foetus, her elbows supported by her thighs, as she chewed anxiously on her fingernails. On the floor were scattered piles of VHS and Betamax cassettes and two video machines. The rectangular black boxes were her escape from the reality of three screaming children. At six years old, I'd watch my mother staring at the television for hours, day after day. She was a body in pyjamas – day and night, with untidy hair and a mask-like, expressionless face. Occasionally, she smiled at the television, but she didn't look happy. I felt less important (and less loved) than the movie characters she appeared to idolise. Cindy, Ralph and I knew not to disturb her. Her emotional absence was easier to deal with than her anger. Mum was there, but we were lonely.

'Mom…'

'Huh?' She would never look up. I would drop my head and walk away.

After losing her parents and sister in quick succession,

she became locked up in her grief. It consumed her mind, leaving no room for her children and making it impossible for her to manage anything else.

'Stop being naughty!' she'd yell at us for just being kids.

As a result, I instinctively adapted to what Mum needed. I feared her rage and believed my behaviour was 'bad.' I felt equally to blame for her sadness and responsible for her happiness. When my mother was hurting, I assumed it was my fault.

This first experience of trauma and loss shaped my self-image and later, my parenting. After losing my father, it would pave my recovery and return to work.

* * *

'I feel horrible telling you these things. You have gone through way worse. I don't feel right burdening you.'

I was astounded by my client Raina's depth of understanding and compassion, as over the years, I'd often questioned her level of insight. I was reminded of the value of remaining open and curious, whilst evaluating another person or situation.

I've always been aware of holding others 'in mind' because of the way my mother struggled to hold me in mind those many years before. Mum wasn't self-centered, she was simply incapable. I know that a secure attachment stems from quality parenting rather than the quantity of time spent with your child. Children of pre-occupied, depressed mothers are more likely to have depression in later life because a depressed mother is less attentive and tends to express anger towards her children.

As a full-time working mother, I never wanted to repeat this pattern in the parenting of my own kids and have always held a space for them at the forefront of my mind. I'd like to believe that my children know – as if by telepathy – what they mean to me. Yet sometimes, they complain and express their pain, disappointment and lack of worth due to my absence in their lives. I find this hurtful because my intentions have, in fact, been the exact opposite. But it's difficult to make it clear to a child who sees the world concretely that their value and your love are not directly proportional to the time you spend with them.

I've tried to explain this to my children.

'You will understand this when you are older, but I understand it's hard for you. It's horrible for me to hear it and to see how it hurts you. I know what it feels like not to have a parent present or involved, and I didn't want to repeat that with you,' I've reassured them. 'Despite my best intentions, it seems I have.'

In these interactions, I have come to realise that my parents did their best and without meaning to, I might have repeated undesired behaviours, recreating patterns in my children's lives, simply in different ways. My dad worked hard to give me a good life, and my mother wasn't around because she had her struggles. I have to believe my children will see my side one day. It's always a balance to try explain my position and manage my guilt (and any indulgent and lax parenting) without invalidating their feelings and furthering their shame for needing time with me. Parenting isn't easy.

Admittedly, after losing Dad, I was struck by how

little I thought about my children. It felt strange, yet uncontrollable, as if my mind simply couldn't hold them whilst I was consumed by my grief. *Was this how Mum had felt?*

Sometimes, people fall apart after losing someone they depend on for support. This, I've come to believe, explains the tragic story of my special uncle, Harry, my mother's brother, whom I loved dearly. He, like my mother, was very close to and reliant on his parents, and sadly turned to alcohol following their deaths. Drinking filled the void and numbed his pain. Unfortunately, his severe drinking problem morphed into full-blown alcoholism which consumed him. It cost him his family – another loss in the domino of tragedies, affecting his wife, children and all of us close to them.

My uncle died tragically only six months after Dad – yet another blow for my poor mother. But he'd proudly overcome his addiction with alcohol and had been sober for seventeen years prior to his passing.

It's tough when someone close to you is struggling emotionally or is unable to be present psychically (or physically – as I am frequently due to work). Their absence might seem self-indulgent, leaving you with uncomfortable emotions – abandonment, rejection, fear, confusion or resentment. It's hard not to judge and also to understand someone else's responses and reactions to loss or trauma, or their reaction to going through a tough time in their lives (or simply, their everyday life choices). Everything is relative.

My approach is that feelings are neither right nor wrong but are an expression of how each of us interprets every situation we face. We are all entitled to our feelings; but when left unexplored or unmanaged, they can negatively influence our self-esteem, responses and further reactions and relationships.

Over time, I've thought back to the double loss I suffered when my father died, and I lost my connection to my Uncle David. I remember reaching out to him after I'd returned to Sydney, desperate to hear some words of comfort after a long day's work. I'd assumed I hadn't heard from him for a while because he was grieving his little brother and speaking to me may have been too triggering for him. But as I'd cried on the phone, he'd responded with the lifeless platitude, 'Death happens to everyone,' without a hint of warmth in his tone. Something between us died right then. I felt no empathy from him for my dad or me.

Since then, I kept trying to see things from his point of view in search of an explanation for his uncharacteristic behaviour. I had so wanted him at my side to support me during my lowest moment. In some ways, my uncle had been more instrumental in my life than even my own father because I'd admired his kindness, graciousness, intellect, success and strong family values.

Three years later, whilst catching up with my cousin, Uncle David's son, I had a major breakthrough. My cousin shared his grief with me about the tragic impact of ageing on his father's brain morphology, cognitive functions and personality, which had been happening for some time. In that moment, I realised that my uncle's indifference was not due to a lack of care or withholding information when my dad died. He simply wasn't well.

Hearing this, I imagined my cousins' grief, having to witness the changes to their father and was overcome with sadness as I remembered the great man my uncle was. In our hearts, he would remain so.

I came to understand that shame and anger had concealed my heartbreak, and I was finally able to lay my secret grudge against my uncle to rest. It was a moment of release in which I exhaled a silent message of acceptance, healing and love, and the wish for a re-establishment of a lost connection with him. He was not the father who had brought me into the world, but the father I had relied on many times to carry me through it.

Looking back, I realise my uncle's behaviour wasn't malicious. It was out of his control, and I had misjudged and misunderstood it. Things had changed over time in both of us, and as a result, so did our relationship. Because of that, I felt I'd lost him. But it had nothing to do with my dad. I had directed my anger at him because I felt he didn't give me the support I needed when Dad died. I was hyper-sensitive and reacted to what I perceived as his lack of emotional availability.

What matters is how these moments of disconnect at crucial times in our lives create division, confusion, mixed responses and trigger our own issues. My uncle's reaction was coincidental and had concurred with me needing someone to be angry at.

In being able to see my uncle more clearly, I've acknowledged the sadness of loss that accompanies the inevitable passage of time on our bodies and minds. My heart breaks for my cousins and aunt as they face loss of a different kind, as is the case when the person we love becomes a shadow of their former selves. I forgive myself for misjudging my uncle's actions. And with that, I am able to love and respect him again.

Trauma causes far-reaching and all-encompassing devastation. Regardless of which side we find ourselves on, it's important to acknowledge this and reach out for help when we need it.

At the same time, we can look back and forgive those who hurt us while they were hurting, understanding that it was their own crushing grief (or other underlying issues) that precluded them from making space for us in their minds. When we understand this, we can begin to repair our wounded self-image that was cast in the shadow of that emptiness.

CHAPTER 18
Living Inside a Bubble

In the first few weeks after I returned to work, I existed in a bubble, like the child from the 1976 John Travolta movie, *The Boy in the Bubble*, who lived in his plastic home. I watched the passing parade through my office windows, completely disconnected from the world outside – everything seemed superficial and pointless. I was suffering from depression. I recognised the many symptoms of the 'Black Dog' I had heard about, and though I knew it couldn't yet be termed 'biological,' I felt it throughout my body and mind.

I felt more real inside my room because it was a safe space to be vulnerable with my clients, but now it was my haven too. It was exposing and frightening to need others in my fragile state, and this brought up my shame and weakness. I did not want to burden anyone. My dormant fears of abandonment resurfaced as I feared being viewed as too needy and rejected as a result. I questioned whether I was worthy of care, reopening closed chapters of my past.

I felt different, otherworldly. Pure. Grief dissolved the layers of my protective defenses that kept me at a healthy distance from others. In this raw state, I understood others' suffering as never before, feeling it deep within my chest. My compassion for others was magnified, transforming my sense of non-verbal communication, where feelings run like currents between humans into a superpower. All human connection seemed magnetic.

I found myself with a new sense of awe for my clients' bravery and trust. Over the years, they had shared their most tender and guarded emotions with me. Now I knew firsthand how exposing that felt, and I was humbled by the privilege and newly respectful of the responsibility. More than ever, I wanted to step up and be there to help them in their times of hardship. Although I did not feel entirely myself, I did my best and allowed the power of shared human experiences and emotions to steer my way.

In my state of trauma, living became reduced to the simplest values of kindness, compassion, connectedness and humility. I was in touch with my mortality and that of others. Never before had the socially constructed divisions between people lacked more substance.

With the superficial layers of life stripped away, I caught glimpses of the purity that exists in all humans, as if we were all vibrating on an otherworldly plane. I imagined it to be what Buddhism refers to as the 'lack of attachment' to possession, emotions and situations. I was able to simply be and to sense the wastefulness of any pretense, materialism or 'doing' if it was not for the greater good of humanity.

I had felt this same sense of connectedness while standing behind Dad's coffin, ready for the procession to his burial site. As I'd surveyed the many somber faces, I couldn't help pondering what it means to live a meaningful life. In that moment, I'd been caught up in the existential, as one tends to be when faced with tragedy, loss, illness or impending death. I struggled to see value beyond my family and my health. Dad had touched our lives in the lessons he'd taught us and the love he'd shared – not in money or possessions, but in his humanity.

After the funeral, my sister shared a mourner's prayer with me. It acknowledged our loss, thanked God and prayed for Dad's soul to be elevated. I was perplexed. I was angry at God (if there was one) for taking Dad from me. Why should I give thanks when we had been robbed in the most horrendous way?

With time I have come to realise that loss emphasises life's plentitude. Although Dad was gone, what remained was my gratitude for the time I had with him. I was thankful for Mum, my children, and family members who are alive and well. I had enough – not everything. The bounty didn't detract from the pain of my loss, but still, I was appreciative of it.

Loss can illuminate gratitude. But they are distinct entities. They cannot be balanced on the same scales. What we have cannot detract from the sadness, disappointment and other negative emotions that accompany grief. We suffer guilt when we try to use appreciation as a Band-Aid for our hurt.

Some of us view emotional pain, or the daily flatline, as failure and will do anything to try and experience continuous happiness and success. It doesn't help that the media supports the narrative that we should achieve rapid results and ignores the endless hard work, setbacks and miseries that are a natural part of every life. We risk being self-destructive in the pursuit of a quick injection of joy.

Eastern philosophy teaches that pain in life is inevitable. Anyone who has experienced trauma and loss knows this to be true. When we are drowning in sorrow, we sometimes have the urge to give up. We grow tired of the endless struggle of swimming against the tide of effort it takes to complete the simplest of tasks. It's exhausting and soul-destroying. For those who have had to overcome repeated hardships, new upsets can cause massive setbacks. The feeling of brokenness raises the terror of never being whole again. Living through the dark tunnel of turmoil is never easy to manage, but it is the only option if we want to reach the other side.

So when Tessa, a dear client, voiced her fear of losing her father, although it was nearly three years after my loss, I resonated with her. By that time, I was stronger and could tolerate her intense pain.

'I don't want to continue without the support. The thought of losing someone scares me. I've had so many breakdowns thinking about losing Dad and waking to a day without him. I go the brink of panic attacks,' she told me.

Tessa is autistic and her lack of independent living meant she was more vulnerable. She relied on her father, and her fears were real and justified. It was as if she was grieving him before he was gone.

Tessa's autism meant she understood loss in concrete terms – from lost objects to broken and irreparable items. The hurt and discomfort of never again seeing or having her important objects close by was hugely challenging for her. Her compromised ability to think in abstract terms made loss even more difficult to digest, manage and accept.

Tessa had begun to monitor her father's every word, movement, memory and lack thereof, and interpreted any deviation as a sign of his impending demise.

'I know it's coming, and I can't stop it,' she cried in my room one day, and I had no way to prevent her darkest thoughts from eventuating.

'There is a space between having something there, and then not having it, that appears so small. But it's massive, and there is so much in between that needs processing,' she told me.

I found her random insights to be an enigma.

'Feeling can be so challenging that sometimes, I numb myself to feel nothing, but then I feel so empty and detached. This is so hard!' Tessa was weeping, covering her eyes, her body twisted as she leaned over the back of the couch, avoiding eye contact with me. I sensed how shamed and awkward she felt.

I felt helpless as I witnessed her agony and tears.

I knew that pain intimately.

And all I could offer was my presence as we sat in the windowless room, sharing her profound sorrow.

CHAPTER 19
Grieving Professionally

I'd sent Linda my usual text-message appointment reminder, but she had not replied. For a second, it crossed my mind that it was out of character for Linda, but I soon moved on from the thought.

'Dr Myers, thank you. I'll be there,' Linda always responded to my message. Her diligence stood out, as clients don't generally reply. I had known Linda since her later years of high school, and she was a thoughtful, kind and respectful young woman. I was proud of her progress and resilience. She had struggled through high school with feelings of being left out, unwanted, different and shameful. She was now a social worker student.

Two days before her upcoming appointment, my phone rang. I don't usually take a call at work if I don't recognise a number to avoid any chance of getting stuck on lengthy calls. Ironically, that day, I answered the phone.

'Hello, Dr Myers, I am Linda's uncle. Her mother has asked me to call you.'

Immediately, I went cold, knowing that something was horribly wrong. He told me that Linda had tragically taken her own life. I broke down in tears. Having lost my father the year before, and with similar questions surrounding the cause of his death, I was simply shattered by the news of Linda's passing.

He tried to provide answers to my questions. We spoke for some time, but I wasn't hearing. My mind raced with thoughts of the many sessions I had had with Linda over the years as she sat across from me in my consulting room.

Although her journey had been tumultuous, she had always managed to pull herself from the depths of her pain into a more rational and thoughtful head space. From that place, she could fight another day, knowing that things weren't perfect but they were manageable and good enough, as she tried to quieten her inner voice that kept telling her she wasn't wanted or good enough. Over the years, I'd generally felt confident that talking to her or tweaking medication, if needed, would bring her out of her emotional pit. During our numerous sessions, she would work through and process her thoughts and emotions, and always left my rooms lighter, more positive and capable of moving forward again. At least, until the next time she stumbled over her feelings, falling backwards into her past beliefs. She, like many others, held years of negative feeling states.

Linda's suicide left me heartbroken. I couldn't stop thinking that if only she had made it to our next appointment – it was only two days away – she might have found the strength to carry on. I could only think that perhaps she didn't want to be 'talked out of it' again. I couldn't be certain my words would have changed her mind. Perhaps my guilt would have been worse had she taken her life immediately following our session?

For some mental health sufferers, acts of harm don't end in death as the ultimate plan, but their impulsive decision unwittingly ends tragically.

That might have been the case with Phil, a troubled young man I met almost exactly a year after Linda's death.

'My son has never wanted therapy,' his mother said to me at our first appointment. She had come alone to prime me and assess whether I would be 'a good fit' for her son.

Phil and I managed to establish some rapport in our two meetings, and he seemed open to talking. He had a challenging relationship with his father and carried the hurt and loss of not having the parent-child relationship he'd needed or wanted. I felt Phil's pain when he spoke and when he was silent. His grief was raw, yet to be processed into words, but I felt hopeful that it was possible. He had taken steps to pick up the fragments of his life. He was working, studying and making progress, but he used substances to numb his pain.

'Phil has sadly lost his battle to his demons,' the text read.

I rang immediately. Phil's mother answered, sobbing. She told me he had most likely taken his life, but they were yet to identify a body. She was still in shock, sounding calm between her intense, unravelled crying spells.

I met the family of both my young clients to offer condolences in the days following their deaths. This is not professionally mandated, but to me, it felt necessary. I was grieving too, having had my own special relationship with both Linda and Phil – clinical and professional, but still warm, caring and close.

'Thank you for everything you did for Linda,' her mother said as we sat around a low coffee table. She had prepared a beautiful spread for our afternoon tea. There were perfectly cut sandwiches, biscuits and a freshly baked cake, but I couldn't eat. I felt undeserving of their food.

Casual greetings were followed by long moments of sadness, regret and disillusionment. Linda's father felt responsible, having last seen her and not 'picked up a thing.' It was difficult to witness his torment. I knew it would haunt him forever. I felt guilty too, not having protected Linda's parents from losing their daughter.

Linda was 'so happy the past few days,' he said.

We discussed the possibility that in those days before her death, she was perhaps at peace with her resolve to end her life, and no longer had to live with the difficult decision to live or die. She was likely relieved, knowing that she would soon be done with her pain forever. I could only imagine Linda's internal battle, knowing the damage her death would inflict upon her family, because she had often spoke about that to me. She had never wanted to hurt them.

A year later, I reached out to her family by text. December always reminds me of my loss, which now includes Linda. Her mother replied, asking to talk, and I readily volunteered time; but I never heard back from her. I assumed her mother's readiness to address her grief fluctuated, as did mine. Timing, when it comes to managing a difficult situation, differs for us all; and it wasn't my place to rush another's process, but rather to walk alongside their grief journey.

Phil's parents expressed gratitude for my time. It felt strange because I was expecting them to be angry. I was struck by Phil's father's depth of pain, and I recalled Phil holding a similar pain at our second and final session. Despite his hurt, Phil's dad, like Phil himself, was pragmatic and enquiring as he asked for factual evidence, medical opinions and concrete answers. I understood his need.

Internally, I deliberated about the information I disclosed, considering the necessity and benefit of sharing the hidden parts of Phil's secret garden with his parents, other than to cause them greater pain. I knew that Phil had needed time to work through his anguish, but we hadn't been granted that time. His grief would remain forever unprocessed and open-ended. I would close Phil's clinical file, but not his story, and nor would his family.

I felt fraudulent supporting these parents, as I could never know their pain; but having lost Dad, I had a small window into their now very dark world. I did my utmost to provide them my time and the space to remember their child, express their hurt and contain it for them for a short while.

'The worst part of this job is losing a client,' I shared with a newly graduated colleague. 'One of the worst was Elena. I still see her parents now and again around Bondi Junction, and every time, I just cry.'

I told the colleague how I had gone to St Vincent's Hospital to see her. Her mother had called to let me know she only had days left to live. I found her lying in bed, eyes closed, delirious from the morphine. I had held her hand and said goodbye. It was so painful. I had looked at her old Yugoslavian grandmother sitting on a big blue chair in the corner of the hospital room. She looked tiny, sucked in by the size of the chair. She spoke no English, but I could see her looking at me and then at Elena; and I knew she was thinking, *This should be me, not my grandchild.*

Elena didn't commit suicide, but she couldn't live with mental illness. Yes, her cancer killed her, but I knew Elena hated being a mortal with flaws. This wasn't due to overt narcissism, but rather covert feelings of guilt and badness, passing on her 'problem' to a husband or crueller, a child.

I attended her funeral. I have done so many times for patients since then. I remember each of them because it is always incredibly difficult. I walked with them, and often knew more intimate details of their suffering than anyone else. And I knew their families, the hardships and the battles often hidden from the world.

I sat silently for a moment and then stood up to leave my colleague's office.

'As the doctor, you're there, but you're not part of the family. It's a weird position, and it makes grieving tough.' My loud thoughts were no longer directed at her.

I reached for the door, pensive and sad, then added, 'The most difficult for me is having to remove their file. I leave it for months because I have to be ready to say goodbye.'

CHAPTER 20

Slow Steps

'My adult cousins and aunt are all still sleeping in the lounge room,' my client Mia said. 'When my uncle couldn't get up the stairs anymore, they all started sleeping downstairs, in the loungeroom, with him.'

Mia was relaying how her extended family was coping with the recent death of her uncle. His cancer and progressive departure had dominated our sessions over the past months. Mia and her uncle had shared a special bond.

'Whenever I was admitted to hospital for my mental health, he would always make the time to visit. He'd come to check on me and wish me well. "You will be great," he'd say. And he'd bring me food that I...' Mia couldn't finish her sentence as tears ran down her cheeks, clearly uncomfortable with the display of the intensity of her emotional response.

I had struggled to hold back my own tears, sitting opposite her in the security of my large blue armchair. I couldn't find appropriate words to say.

Mia continued, smiling awkwardly. 'My cousins and aunt won't even remove his bed – it's a hospital bed! It's in the middle of the loungeroom! Where are guests meant to sit?'

I could see that she wanted me to confirm that this was strange behaviour, but I refrained.

'What if someone else might need the bed? Oh, and it's rented. And my family and other relatives are paying for it by the day.'

Because it was taking up the entire living room, Mia judged her cousins and aunt's decision to hold on to the bed in which their father had died. While she spoke, I thought of my mother's obsession with holding on to her parents' furniture.

Finally, I spoke. 'I suppose we all manage these situations differently. Your uncle died only two weeks ago. It's still so soon for your cousins and aunt. I imagine their letting go will be a gradual process so that they can continue their lives without him.'

'Yeah,' Mia agreed. Finally, able to offer herself compassion, perhaps not yet consciously, she continued. 'I found it hard to have an ordinary Father's Day this weekend. Usually, we would see my uncle. The family wanted a group Zoom call. I didn't feel up to it. In fact, I didn't feel up to doing much.' She looked so sad. Her eyes were glassy. Mia wasn't one to show much emotion – it was one of the reasons she was seeing me.

'Maybe you too are going to need time before things feel back to normal again?' I suggested.

As Mia fought her emotions, she drifted away for a

moment. Perhaps it was dawning on her that her family's need to hold on to her uncle's bed a little longer wasn't that odd.

Later, I reflected on the first few weeks after Dad's death. I'd arrived in Sydney, so happy to see my children, home and friends. Although everything was familiar, I was different. I was unnerved by my enormous feelings of fear and fragility because I'd always been so strong. I had the grit and determination to override my fatigue and forfeit opportunities that would allow me to let go and enjoy life. I had always known how to operate my ambition to deliver success. The downside of this personality trait – as with any trait when the unregulated upsides become destructive – was that in the past I'd turned down being present for meaningful events (including funerals), ignored my health, often fell ill and disappointed people by overcommitting and being unable to deliver to my promises.

Losing Dad sapped my strength; and for weeks, maybe months, I was depressed and lacked motivation. For many years, I'd always hopped out of bed at the first beep of my alarm and raced to the gym. Now I could barely lift my head off the pillow, and when I managed to do that, I had no desire. Nothing made me happy.

'I'm sorry, Shelby. I just can't train. I need time,' I told my gym trainer of eight years.

'Take your time, Lisa. There is no rush.' She was young but exhibited a deep understanding, which I'd always admired. Shelby's personal tragedies had made her empathetic and wise, beyond the expectations of her chronological age.

Though I felt depressed, I was suffering from grief. It resembled depression in that I felt flat and low in mood. Nothing I previously enjoyed made me feel happy. I wasn't motivated to exercise or socialise. I wanted to be alone. I felt hopeless. I wasn't able to fall asleep at night but felt glued to my bed in the morning. Food was something I needed rather than wanted. There were moments I felt better and more myself, but without a warning or trigger, I'd slump again.

The symptoms of grief tend to fluctuate, differentiating it from depression. It comes in waves, so there are times when you can feel quite fine and more yourself again.

During those months, I operated at the most basic level of mothering, doctoring and partnering as I struggled to be fully present. At work, my default was to be clinical, somewhat robotic, as I listened, managed any risk issues, performed adequate assessments and wrote necessary prescriptions and plans for clients' care needs. I was analytical and practical as I waited for the signs of my readiness to plunge into deeper waters again, to reappear.

My decision to step back was partially conscious. I knew I lacked my usual strength and capacity; but I didn't realise that in doing so, I was also acknowledging my hurt, brokenness and the time I needed to heal. I was finally able to show myself self-kindness and tolerance that I've seldom been able to access in my nature.

When I realised I was floundering, I decided to return to therapy. I couldn't manage and compress my feelings. I should have returned sooner, but I was afraid of opening myself and falling to pieces in the process. It was all I could do to hold myself together. It was easier to block everything than to try talk about it.

Though I'd had a therapist for eight years, I looked for a new one. My dissatisfaction with my current therapist was a reaction to my frustration with life. I wasn't happy in myself and projected my dissatisfaction onto my therapist, believing I needed someone else to do a better job at 'fixing' me and my life. I soon realised how wrong I was, sitting in front of someone who felt like a stranger. She simply didn't know all the bits and pieces of my story, and that lack of familiarity left too much missing in our connection. Of course, it wasn't her fault.

Finally, I reconnected with my original therapist, bringing my heavy load of grief-stricken and angry baggage. She gave me permission to express it all, which relieved me. I needed a safe space to have difficult conversations. I couldn't wait for my hour with her so I could re-anchor and recalibrate for the week ahead. In front of her, I opened the messy wardrobe that held my 'stuff,' unpacked everything, cried and raged, before repacking it in an organised way until my following session. That process allowed me to function day to day.

Moving on from trauma or loss is a slow, lengthy and complicated process, and it is different for everyone. A useful analogy is to think of recovery from an operation or physical injury. It takes time to get well. You need to start slowly, take tiny steps and return to basics. You start by walking, then walk-running and finally, you begin to run again.

When something inside us breaks, the recovery is more difficult because the injury is invisible. We might think our feelings are silly, indulgent, not to be taken seriously.

Emotional pain can't be easily fixed with a pill, stitch, pin or plate. Regaining our full pre-trauma functioning takes time. It is a convoluted journey with many ups and downs along the way.

It is like climbing up a ladder, each rung represents a stage in the process. Our progress is best gauged when we look down and can see how far we have come. We may struggle to recognise how much further we have to go because without complete self-awareness, we can't gauge the unknown. We might always feel as if we are in the right place of our journey, and I imagine that is because in fact, we are. Our responses to the same situation can also change as we move through different phases. In my case, I had to deal with the trauma of my father's death before I could truly mourn him.

Many of us experience or have already faced multiple catastrophic moments of breakdown in our lives, from postnatal depression, to overcoming perfectionism, emigration, divorce and the death of people we love. Having experienced all of these before I lost my dad, I believed I was managing my dad's death fairly well. I realised months and years later that I was wrong. I had been operating on autopilot, largely avoiding the enormity of my grief. Grief, you see, like many things in life, cannot be controlled.

Hindsight gave me a far clearer perspective.

CHAPTER 21
The Good-Enough Parent

I stood motionless in disbelief within the tiny cubicle and felt the closeness of old white walls lined with glossy square tiles. Seeking certainty, I walked briskly to the nurses' station, my steps in tune with the beat of my heart.

'Sister, do you see one or two lines here?' I put the white plastic pregnancy test under her nose.

She looked puzzled and answered, seemingly annoyed, 'Doctor, there are two lines. The person is pregnant.'

That person was me! I shoved the test into my handbag and took a seat in the circle of simple hard wooden chairs laid out for our morning ward round. Surrounded by colleagues holding their files, I sat gripping my bag on my lap. I heard nothing, unable to concentrate. I kept looking at the test that sat mounted on my personal belongings in the bag. Perhaps it might miraculously change to a single line. *I am not ready to be pregnant! How will I cope? I'm so afraid! I need to call Dad.*

When the meeting was barely concluded, I jumped up and raced outside. Pacing the gravel driveway of one of the many face-brick buildings at Sterkfontein Hospital which detained involuntary patients too unwell to be housed at any other mental health facility across Johannesburg, I called Dad as I did whenever I didn't know what to do. As always, he soothed my fears. 'That's amazing news, Lisa. We will all help. You will be fine. It's such great news.'

Dad is right. It is great news. I am about to become a mother.

Being pregnant with my first child, I was consumed with anxieties. Immediately, I worried that my life would be thrown off its perfect course and feared becoming mentally ill. Being a psychiatry registrar, I was yet to complete my training, and pregnancy wasn't part of my plan, nor did it align with my drive to succeed or have any room within my obsessive work ethic. I worried I wouldn't have enough time to study and achieve the results I was accustomed to whilst caring for a child.

After the initial shock wore off, I slowly absorbed the idea of a baby and began planning how he or she would slot into *my* life. 'I will take the baby to the gym and have the bassinet next to the treadmill.'

My sister scoffed at me. 'Yeah, right!'

I simply ignored her, refusing to accept that someone (especially a little baby) would force me to change my ways.

In the safe space of my own therapy, I often brought up my fear about becoming mentally ill.

I'm worried I'll become psychotic. 'Pregnancy and childbirth can do that,' I said, offloading my anxiety onto my therapist. 'My mother had postnatal depression when my older sister was born.'

I considered my fears justified, but perhaps, I had too much knowledge from studying and working in mental health. As a psychiatry registrar, the more educated I became about the huge range of mental health issues that can derail a person's life, the more nervous I grew about suffering from them myself. I was terrified of the impact of genetics given my own family's history of postnatal depression (PND). Mum had often spoken about her time as a new mother and how overwhelmed, depressed and riddled with anxiety she'd become to the point that she couldn't take care of my sister. Dad had to take over all the childcare. When he had to go to work, his mother would come over to babysit Cindy. One day, Mum was told by her doctor that if she didn't 'snap out of it,' she'd need to be hospitalised. Hearing these words somehow snapped her back into gear. I'm not sure how that worked, but she has stood by that story. So if my mother couldn't manage her firstborn due to severe anxiety, what would happen to me when I became a mother?

As if only yesterday, my firstborn Daniella lay wrapped in a multi-coloured flannel blanket, asleep on my naked chest after a Caesarean section. For many new mothers, this might have been a moment of quiet bliss, but not for me. I instantly became panicked that she wasn't following the prototypical behaviour of a newborn.

'Why is she not sniffing for milk? Should I wake her and put her on the breast?' I fretted, firing questions at the recovery nurse who casually attended to her notes.

In the weeks that followed, I experienced an avalanche

of unwanted experiences, which solidified my inadequacy as a mother and woman. I had been unable to have a natural birth and struggled to breastfeed, and as a result, I felt useless. Seeing friends cope with their babies only made me feel worse.

I spent the first six weeks post birth in a fog, walking around my home in my pyjamas. My world narrowed to visits from midwives and lactation consultants, whilst I read books and collected opinions on how to latch a newborn, get her to sleep and wake in forty-five-minute blocks and obsessed over feeding her the exact amount of milk per kilo body weight.

Neurotic and frustrated, I flung my inadequacy together with my nipple shields, which helped me latch my baby, at everyone who couldn't fix it and everything that was causing it – a slight noise, a too-bright light or a feed that didn't go well.

One morning, as I stood in the kitchen, dishevelled due to a lack of sleep, my mum looked at me and said, 'Lisa, you need to take something, or see someone – you are not coping.'

I wasn't coping. She was right. I wasn't coping at all. How was this possible? I always coped and always succeeded. I wasn't a failure. I never failed. I was meant to be perfect.

In many ways – and this is difficult to admit – motherhood felt unnatural to me. I'd been a free, strong woman, and having to be home-bound with this little thing so dependent on me was a challenge. In deeper psychological terms, I was struggling with the idea of someone needing me when I wasn't comfortable with my own neediness of others. From a young age, due to my mother's uncontained emotions and unprocessed trauma, I had learnt to suppress my needs or alternatively, manage them by over-achieving.

Struggling with breastfeeding, I eased my overwhelming anxiety and embarrassment with large chocolate McDonald's milkshakes that I'd 'treat' myself to every day, alongside a big 'healthy' muffin. I'd convinced myself that I was breastfeeding and needed additional calcium. One day, my sister-in-law, a dietician, told me that powdered chocolate with skim milk would be a healthier option. *Seriously, how was that going to treat my depression?*

As my weight increased, I cursed the textbooks that claimed breastfeeding helped you lose the weight put on during pregnancy.

Looking back now, I can see that my obsession with postnatal problems was a guise for my deeper issue – fear of losing control. I'd always been able to obsessively regulate my life and lived by schedules and lists. This predictability made me feel safe. I didn't have to need anything or anyone. I could manage it all and at the same time, achieve and be recognised for it.

I'm not atypical. We all strive for some power in our lives. We discover early in life that having order over our environment, and those who are in it, provides us with feelings of safety. Humans are wired towards survival, and achieving security is instinctual. The more out of control we feel (whether consciously or not) during stages of our life, the more likely our emergent deep-seated anxieties fuel our need to contain the external world.

I have always feared falling apart. Until I became a new mother, I'd been able to suppress my abundant emotions, disable my stop button and push through without ever acknowledging my fears and flaws. The terror of my own vulnerability was another factor driving my need to command my environment. When we're not yet aware of or comfortable with our vulnerability, we seek to manage ourselves and how we appear to the outside world. Superficially, we can present as capable and powerful, whilst hiding and denying our sense of uselessness.

Before becoming a mother, I denied any vulnerability and felt disgust at my own needs. Learning to tolerate – and finally, embrace and even love – my weaknesses was a real turning point in my personal development.

During my training to become a psychiatrist, I took pride in the fact that I always put immense pressure on myself to do *everything* just right and perfect. There was no taking it easy. I never took breaks. There was no letting up. It was go, go, go; and as a result, I subconsciously thought that if I could expect this level of work from myself, I could expect it from everyone around me. In an assessment, one of the consultants remarked that I appeared intolerant of my colleagues. He noted that I was smart, hardworking and able to do things quickly and effectively; but at the same time, I would get frustrated with those around me whom I perceived as weak or unable to do things the way I did. He saw right through my defences and accurately identified my discomfort with vulnerability and imperfection.

As a mother, I was brought to a screeching halt – a tiny being had the power to push me off my pedestal and force me to confront my fragility and fears of incompetence. How grateful I am now for that experience and its impetus to create such a radical shift within me and promote immense personal growth. But to grow, like to grieve, is a boundless process. To this day, I still find it challenging having to moderate the expectations I have for myself and those around me (and any feelings of failure).

I lived the first part of my life trying to conceal my family's lack of education and errors, my religion and who I was. Having a child first brought to light and forced me to confront my sense of defectiveness. Over the years, I have evolved my sense of self, alongside my values and my mistakes. The more I've shaped and grown comfortable with myself, the easier it has become to stand alone, yet not feel lonely, knowing what I stand for. I have let go of my need to compare, put down and envy others as life has become a race against myself.

Perhaps you're wondering: what is our *sense of self*?

It's the internal idea of who we are, how we feel about ourselves and what we believe others think about us. It's the qualities that define us, and it incorporates our feelings of purpose and meaning in the world.

Let me use an example: due to my deep insecurities and fears of annihilation, I have strived to achieve and build things around me because they make me feel secure. The layman's idea of narcissism is of someone who is completely self-absorbed, in love with themselves and feels better than anyone else in every way. But in truth, being narcissistic is a defence and a means of protecting (sometimes through denying or concealing) a weak, defenceless, shameful, worthless self, whether we recognise it or not. Many of us have these narcissistic defences to a greater or lesser degree, of course. They shield us against crumbling and falling into mounds of nothingness when we confront our feelings of being 'less than,' 'unlovable' or 'not good enough.'

My narcissistic defences have influenced my need to achieve, feel useful, be recognised as the rescuer and always be the best at everything I do. Strangely, with such a strong inner critic, I am most competitive with myself. My achievements and recognition from others allow me to feel good enough at times. But 'imposter syndrome' has certainly been woven into my neuro-circuitry, and I often grapple with feeling fraudulent and not really the capable person I present to the world. Achieving success has validated my fragile self and given me a way to be independent of others. This has served to put out the fires on my fears to survive.

Years after I thought I had conquered these demons, Dad's death brought my shame back to the boil, making it impossible for me to hide my family behind my achievements. His dubious death, the unanswered questions and rumours that ensued were eerily ironic, but they forced me to take another step towards shameless freedom. I acknowledged that my father's actions weren't mine. Neither did I need to 'rubbish' him by projecting my insecurity-driven tendency to find fault. I could accept him as a whole person without judgement. I could still love a man who had erred. He remains a wonderful person and father. Giving up my pretence around my father has allowed me to develop a tolerance for my own imperfections. Like my daughters have been my greatest teachers, so too was Dad to me in his death.

Dad was good enough, and I want that sentiment to resonate into the universe with the knowledge that I will forever be honoured to be known as 'Sam's daughter.'

I hope I'm able to leave my daughters with a similar legacy.

CHAPTER 22

Making Space for Anger

When she was five years old, I walked into Daniella's bedroom to find her packing a suitcase. She was only slightly bigger than the purple-tinted, partially torn fabric container that once held her happiest memories. I stood in front of her, but she refused to look up at me. She was focusing her complete attention on ensuring she had gathered every necessary belonging to live without me.

'I hate you. I am not staying with you. I am going to Dad,' she said in a firm voice. I was pierced by the anger of her pain, and I begged her to stay.

'Please don't go, Dani. I'm so sorry for hurting you. I love you.' I felt empty, knowing I couldn't fix her broken world.

'Well, I don't love you.' Her words stung.

I had imagined my marriage would last forever. I did not foresee or plan ending it when my daughters were only five and two-and-a-half years old. It was the most devastating event of my life at the time – I hadn't yet lost my father. On the surface, my divorce was a failed relationship; but on a deeper and more significant level, it signalled the breaking up of a home, and it robbed my children of an intact traditional nuclear family – the kind kids want, no matter how unhappy their parents are.

Ironically, while I was growing up, I'd often wished – even begged – my parents to separate. I spent frustrated years upset, terrified and miserable, being forced to listen to their constant arguing, yelling and flinging of nasty words at one another. However, my parents remained married, so I will never truly know whether I'd have been happier if they'd divorced.

A few years ago, Daniella shared with me her vivid memory of the moment her father and I told her of our plans to separate. I, on the other hand, have no recollection of it. Maybe I blocked it out or wasn't able to be attentive enough to my children as much as I am ashamed to admit this. Her account of that day brought me to tears, as I visualised a little five-year-old absorbing the devastating news. Daniella had been petrified and confused, but in my mind, she had seemed so much more mature and capable of taking in the information we were giving her. She appeared to accept the responsibility of having to be the caretaker for her little sister, Rachel. Now I wish I could go back and hold her in that moment and allow her to be just a five-year-old whose world was collapsing.

The entire experience remains a blur – I was focused on going through the motions and couldn't be emotionally present. My mind was in turmoil throughout.

I remain deeply remorseful for the pain and loss

I brought upon my children, which went against my instincts as a protective mother. Our decision to separate was tough. I had to weigh up the pain of living a life of unhappiness, losing myself and exposing my children to an unsatisfactory relationship in which I had become a fraction of their mother against the trauma of breaking up a home and family, which would cause my children heartache with potentially long-term mental health implications (including depression, anxiety and more). I was also terrified of the hardships of becoming a single parent. Steven had his own list of considerations.

Relationships are complicated, and there is no single or exact rule for dealing with all people in all situations. Steven and I have worked hard to shield our children from our dysfunction. We have always made them our priority. I am grateful for his commitment and support. He has always tried his best to be a great dad to the girls. He's had to work hard to overcome his own demons, accept his contribution and try forgiving me for the part I played in destroying his idea of a perfect union, as have I.

As a result of our divorce, Daniella and Rachel have developed the twin qualities of resilience and vulnerability.

Steven and I impressed on them that our failed marriage was not their fault. My philosophy for protecting them stemmed from exactly that – it was what we wanted, not them. Unfortunately, they were stuck in our mess. Children always are.

Ending a relationship doesn't necessarily resolve the destructive dynamics between people. Sometimes, they can be aggravated when matters have to be negotiated through additional layers of anger and resentment.

Unfortunately, despite our best efforts, we sometimes succumb to maladaptive means to avenge our acrimony.

Through the divorce and the months and years that followed, I worked hard to protect my children from the fallout. I spent many hours in therapy, thinking and talking about them as I contemplated their thoughts, emotions and potential subconscious 'drivers' of their behaviour. I did my best to step outside my sadness and guilt, not allowing my inner child to over-identify with their feelings of hurt and abandonment. I had to remain objective when looking into their worlds, which meant I had to hold my feelings whilst simultaneously acknowledging and containing theirs. They needed sincere and sufficient acknowledgement of their suffering, but at the same time, I had to uphold my boundaries.

We went through difficult and scary times, including one incident after a long day when a tired Daniella, who was six years old at the time, became increasingly defiant and unkind towards me. I'd treated children with Oppositional Defiant Disorder and her techy, argumentative manner felt similar. Nothing obvious on that day triggered the onset of her sudden prickliness as I became the recipient of her word-daggers.

'I hate you. Leave me alone. I wish you weren't my mother.'

I could feel my frustration mounting as her verbal attacks kept coming, and I raised my voice, becoming equally combative, 'Don't speak to me like that! Don't be rude, be respectful. I'm your mother! There *will* be a consequence if this continues, Daniella!'

She clenched her fists and screamed with pursed

lips, trying to keep it together, straining to regulate her overwhelming emotions. I watched her dig her nails into her legs and scrunch her eyes to rid herself of her pain.

In that moment, I sensed her desperation. I recognised her suffering and powerlessness, and immediately backed down. She was inflicting physical hurt to manage her emotional pain, and I was momentarily terrified that it might develop into a full-blown personality disorder down the line – all because I, as her mother, could not validate her emotions.

Instantly, I caught myself. I used a calm and soothing voice to de-escalate the situation. I couldn't fix Daniella's broken world, but I could listen, understand and empathise. I could offer love and holding.

'It's okay, sweetheart. It's okay,' I soothed. 'I know this is all so hard for you. I am sorry you have this pain, but I will always love you and be here for you.'

Her screams turned to rapid shallow breaths and then into profound sobs. Finally, an embrace as we sat on the edge of the bathtub, her head burrowed into my chest. I let out a massive sigh and then cried, sharing the hurt and deep pain of our mutual loss and grief.

I would hate to make it seem that simple because it was not. The post-divorce turmoil went on for many, many months – possibly years. Daniella had always been a mommy's girl, but in her hurt and resentment, she drifted from me and began to reject any closeness. She avoided talking to, hugging or kissing me, and shunned even the simplest forms of touch.

So I enlisted the help of a child therapist, Marie, a lovely Canadian woman. Daniella thankfully formed a connection with her, and Marie became my gateway back to my daughter. I would join in their sessions every so often to 'chat to Marie,' whilst in fact directing my words to Daniella, knowing that she was overhearing everything I said.

'It's confusing for her,' Marie would say, offering me insight into my child's inner landscape. 'She is very hurt and feels responsible.'

I both needed to hear this, and at the same time, didn't want to hear it because I hated knowing the extent of her anguish.

The multiparty sessions, three-way conversations, games and puppet shows allowed me to broach certain topics that Daniella angrily shunned when I brought them up with her. 'Marie, Steven and I will always be the girls' parents. We love Dani and Rachel so, so much. And we care for each other, but sometimes, as you know, people don't always work out,' I'd say.

I prayed these reassurances would stick with Daniella and comfort her.

It took a while, but eventually, Daniella's anger slowly melted. She began to ignore me less and her snarls and barks of, 'Don't touch me. I hate you!' or cries of, 'I want to kill myself!' became minimal. I was so relieved.

Only many years later was I able to finally reflect on the benefits of my efforts. I had allowed Daniella to direct her anger at me, whilst tolerating and containing it. This helped her to process and heal. I'd remained firm but loving and understanding of the fact that I had taken away her 'known' world – her family. I took responsibility for it all. It was not appropriate for me, as the adult, to inflict guilt for the hurt she caused me, or force her to understand my needs or burden her with the responsibility of protecting my feelings. Adults have to be adults. Children must be allowed to be children. Adults are there to help children when both parties are suffering.

Nothing felt better than to hold my little girl once again.

My girls still find endings difficult, be it the end of a school year, change of friendships or moving houses. I always acknowledge the pain that can accompany change and support their need for space and time to heal so they can get closure.

How hard life can be, especially when as parents, we are juggling everyone's feelings – including our own – and trying our best to avoid anyone's getting shattered.

With the divorce, I knew it was my role as the mother to buffer my children's emotions at the expense of my own. Breaking up our family and ending my relationship crushed me, but it also crushed my children.

But like most difficulties from which we eventually heal, I have been able to draw from it when empathizing and assisting clients in a similar position. These life lessons, whilst traumatic at the time, have proved invaluable. They have enriched my craft and compassion more deeply than any book or second-hand story ever could.

CHAPTER 23
Supporting Children's Grief

'Grandma Sylvia has gone away, but if you pray really hard, she will come back,' my Aunt Adina told me when I asked where my grandmother had gone.

I was three, and my mother's mother had just died. As a little person, I was confused by my grandmother's sudden absence and a home full of crying, distressed strangers. Interestingly, I didn't ask my mother about my granny's whereabouts. Even at that age, I knew she was absent and floundering as her life collapsed around her.

It's never easy or comfortable explaining death to a child. Adults don't want to contribute to their hurt and often, don't know what a child can understand, absorb and process about a mystery as inexplicable and painful as death.

The next morning, I walked into my aunt's bedroom, hopped into bed between her and my uncle and said, 'I prayed all night, but Grandma Sylvia isn't back.'

Given that I was only a toddler, my aunt's response

was forgivable, though she has since admitted the silliness. She assumed I'd simply accept her words and somehow forget my grandmother as if I was a goldfish with no memory. Adults don't always take children seriously and sometimes treat them as non-humans without depth of feeling, thinking and soul.

Although it's tough, I advocate being truthful when explaining death to a child. But when I got the news of my father's death, I didn't know how I was going to tell my girls because of the horrific circumstances. I have a clear memory of that awful time. Daniella had been out shopping with a friend when Steven collected them early and insisted on dropping her friend home before returning to my place. This confused Daniella who sensed subterfuge. She told me afterwards that she'd assumed it was a surprise visit from my father.

The children came home, bouncing with excitement, followed closely by Steven. I stood up from the couch where I sat next to my mother, my eyes red and puffy.

'What's wrong, Mum?' they asked in chorus.

I'd had minimal time to plan and no experience to guide me in this moment. I cringed as I prepared to deliver the shocking news, anticipating their responses with terror. I knew how much they loved my father. Their innocence had already been partially stripped by living through their parent's divorce. It felt cruel and unfair.

I'm so sorry, girls,' I paused.

Again, they asked what was wrong, intuiting the dread that hung like a black fog in the room. Eventually, I let my mouth emit the mortifying words glued at the back of my throat. 'I'm so, so terribly sorry, but Pa is dead.' It was a scene in slow motion, the stillness of disbelief as I took an audible breath and finally said, 'He's... been killed.'

Rachel had screamed and let out a cry of disbelief, 'No, no, no. It's not true. You are lying. Tell me you're lying.'

She'd refused to be held or consoled. Daniella, initially shocked and quiet, soon became equally hysterical. It took time to ease their overwhelm and confusion. They were insistent, begging me – or someone – to change their new reality. As a mother, I had been tormented, helpless to remedy their heartbreak.

In the hours that followed, they found the crowds of visitors who arrived to comfort us in our home difficult to manage.

'Why are they here when they don't know Pa?' Daniella asked, exasperated.

I explained that they had come to offer us support, but Daniella found it stifling, confronting and confusing. She needed space to quietly process what had happened.

'I want to be alone,' she said.

Retreating to her room, she'd written that letter which she later gave me to read at Dad's funeral and had selected photos of them together and placed them on her bedhead and bedroom walls.

It has been painful to witness how much my daughters, niece and nephew have struggled with the loss of their Pa. Dad was an incredible grandfather. He had unique and intimate relationships with each grandchild. Each one of them has processed their grief differently. My girls tend to internalise their emotions, but when they feel overwhelmed and unable to contain their distress, they sometimes reach out to me.

Months after my father's death, Daniella called me from school.

'Mum!' I could hear the pain in her voice. She began to cry and between her sobs, explained that she'd had to excuse herself from the classroom when her teacher asked the class to discuss their grandparents. There have been other occasions where she has called me in a moment of being triggered and distraught, usually when she sees her friends with their grandparents, hears them talking about being at an event with their grandparents or watches a movie about grandparents. She gets overwhelmed on his birthday and the *Yahrzeit* of his death. As the eldest grandchild, she shared the most time with my father; and her longing, emptiness and agony are painfully evident at these times.

Of her Pa, she says, 'We were very open with each other, Pa and I. We just got each other, and I felt special being the eldest grandchild. We understood each other and never fought. Pa was down to earth and basic. He didn't need much and that made me balanced and gave me perspective. He really made me happy. The little things he did, I didn't appreciate then, but do now – like riding on his scooter and playing school. He knew what to say, and he would play for hours.'

My father always made time to play my daughters' preferred games and got to know them in their space and on their terms. It was his special gift, ensuring that he was familiar with our lives and the people in it. Whenever we spoke, he would always say things like, 'Oh, yes, I know so and so. They are the person who was with you at...'

His interest made us feel important. We knew he

cared. Dad was self-sacrificing and patient with his time, always putting family ahead of himself.

One day, Daniella confessed, 'I saw Grandpa's office. I sent myself the video you had on your phone. Grandpa didn't deserve that pain and suffering.'

I was horrified and reprimanded her for being secretive. I blamed myself for not hiding these confronting images and leaving them accessible on my phone. I asked her how she'd felt seeing them, and she repeated, 'He didn't deserve it. He was a good person.'

I didn't want to push her, so I simply said, 'I'm here if you want to talk about it. I still really struggle when I think about it.' Often, the best we can do is to remind our children and those we care about that we are available, and then be present when they reach out.

Though Rachel had less time with my father, she still had a bond with him. As the family's listening ear, she was often left alone with my distraught mother who was living with us after I returned to work and Daniella was off with friends or in her room. Her grief struck somatically.

'I'm so sore, Mum. My legs are hurting, my hamstrings. And my back. And I have such a bad headache,' Rachel would cry in agony, begging for relief. So I engaged a physiotherapist to massage her grieving body a few times a week.

One day, he called me, concerned. In their session, she'd spoken about how her grandfather had been killed. Was it true? He wanted to know. He wasn't sure what to make of it.

I appreciated his diligence in seeking clarity and explained that it was sadly exactly the case, and was the reason Rachel needed his help. Not being a talker, she was often in physical pain. I explained that I wanted her to take her time with the grieving process and how much the massages were helping to relax her. I asked him to please keep me updated if anything she ever said worried him.

Age doesn't negate the need to process loss. Ralph relayed that one day his son Ethan, my nine-year-old nephew, had put on one of my father's suits – a 1980s-style grey jacket and pants that Ralph had taken after Dad's passing. The suit was ridiculously oversized, but it didn't drown his obvious pride. He asked his dad to take him to Pa's gravesite so he could place a stone there and show his respects.

My children were heartbroken not to be in South Africa for Dad's funeral. But I made the unilateral decision to leave them behind in Sydney – it was my way of protecting them. In hindsight, perhaps, this was a mistake. Being there might have given them necessary closure they have struggled to achieve. They were privy to many hard conversations about my father's death but have since reassured me that it was helpful for them to know everything, rather than be kept in the dark. We gave them enough space to talk and ask questions. I often worry about the impact Dad's death has had or may still have on them. Only time will tell how they have each processed this trauma. In the meantime, all I can do is continue to monitor their emotions and offer support in whatever way I can when I think they are struggling. I can't change the circumstances of Dad's death, but I can help mother my children through the pain his death has wrought.

Grandparents are a valuable part of a child's life. I lost

my grandparents young and felt the void of their absence while I was growing up to such an extent that I prioritised my children having frequent contact and developing a close bond with my parents. I regularly paid for my parents to fly from Cape Town to Johannesburg and, later, to Sydney, to spend time with my daughters. Now more than ever, knowing the fragility of life and the brevity of time, I value my mother's presence in our lives. Since Dad died, Mum has become our beacon of unconditional love and a supportive anchor.

Things changed for everyone the day Dad died. I lost my parenting compass, as I'd often revert to Dad for advice. A difficult decision was always easier when he gave me confirmation that it was the right one. He was a voice of reason for the children whenever they refused to hear mine.

But somehow, I know that when I need his advice, I just need to go inwards and connect with his spirit, and wonder, 'What would Dad do?'

CHAPTER 24

Rebuilding a Broken Home

'Your relationship won't survive emigration.'

The marriage counsellor offered her opinion, having sat quietly, patiently listening whilst Steven and I argued in front of her as if she were invisible. We were ardently trying to convince her who was right so the other one of us could be wrong. Despite her advice, we emigrated as a young family from South Africa to Australia in 2009. I was six months pregnant with Rachel, with a two-and-a-half-year-old Daniella. I was jobless and had to requalify, which entailed studying many hours, leaving Steven to care for the children, which made him increasingly frustrated.

Emigration wasn't the sole reason our marriage ended, but it stressed an already strained relationship.

Emigrating was a mammoth loss. Having to farewell our home, family, friends and country unleashed untold pain. Friends had emigrated before us, but I'd failed to appreciate the immensity of the move. A few years prior to leaving South Africa, my good friend Flo emigrated to Canada.

She'd also been my lactation consultant when Daniella was born, and her patience and non-judging attitude helped me to feel less of an inadequate failure when I was unable to latch and breastfeed my newborn.

'Lis, we are moving to Canada!' Flo announced one day.

'When?' I asked, shocked and secretly hoping it wouldn't eventuate.

'Soon, we have been planning for a while. Sorry, I haven't wanted to tell anyone. It's so hard.'

A month later, Flo stood teary at my front door, saying goodbye. She seemed heartbroken. I hugged her for a last time. Closing the door, I was perplexed by her obvious devastation, imagining the opportunity to live in Canada would only inspire excitement. But when the time came for us to finally leave South Africa, I thought about Flo. I felt guilty that I had not adequately empathised and supported her because I did not appreciate the magnitude of her loss and pain. I felt stupid for not recognizing her emptiness and all-consuming anxiety as she contemplated starting her life over in a foreign country minus her family and friends.

When we flew from Johannesburg to Sydney for the first time, I became claustrophobic and sat on the floor in the tiny space in front of our three economy-class seats. 'I need oxygen, please. I can't breathe, and I am very nauseous.' I was hunched over my pregnant belly, literally feeling sick with grief and terrified of the unknown ahead. At least Steven, Daniella and I had each other.

These memories made the pain of ending a marriage linger long after the actual divorce. My feelings fluctuated, as happens with grief and loss. Steven had been my first real relationship before he became my husband. I hadn't dated other people in my teens and early twenties.

So after our divorce, it was daunting to be a single woman again at forty-something. I had a very different tick-box to my twenty-year-old self, and I came with two children, which I soon discovered, narrowed my options. I began to realise how important it is to have self-assurance and be able to live alone.

Ending our marriage was the right choice, but my certainty frequently wavered, particularly in the years immediately following the divorce. I so missed having the family unit we had lost. I felt sad for my children, but when I met and dated other people, I realised no-one was perfect in a relationship. Distance from my marriage, combined with the impact of my guilt, feelings of failure and the sadness of loss, made me question whether it was really *that* bad. I worried about how others might judge me; after all, it's human nature for those who know us to hold personal opinions. I reminded myself that no-one truly knew my situation, and their thoughts didn't define me. I tried to keep an open mind and listen to helpful and relevant feedback from trusted friends and people whose opinions I respect so that I could grow.

In any marriage, there are always two people who are co-contributors to a flawed dynamic. All relationships go through their good and bad times. Having young kids who require endless attention puts stress on all couples. Everyone is tired, under-appreciated and resentful.

Steven and I finally decided to end our marriage when we both recognised our incompatibility and that neither of us would ever compromise on our divergent lists of non-negotiables. I owned my mistakes, which I knew would become short-lived conversation pieces. But the thought that our failed relationship had become others' dinner-party gossip sparked my paranoia and deep-seated shame. No-one but me and Steven were privy to the deeper issues which finally cleaved us apart. The pain I'd felt in the darker times of our relationship and the guilt for how I'd chosen to manage it would haunt me for years to come. I had to forgive my errors of judgement and remind myself that I was only human.

I'd already spent years in therapy, reflecting on my past, which helped me understand who I was in a relationship and the possible reasons for how events between us unfolded. Since childhood, I had been labelled a problem. My closeness to my father created a triangulation between me, him and my mother; and she frequently blamed me for their marital failings, telling me I was horrible, selfish and unsupportive of her. I know Mum wasn't trying to hurt me – I had never wanted to betray her. But in idealizing my father, I was blinded, and I always took his side. Dad, without malice, manipulated this dynamic to his advantage, instilling in me the belief that Mum was the sole reason for his unhappiness. As a child, I couldn't challenge his flawed theory because I didn't understand how complex relationships are.

I don't blame Steven for what happened to us as a couple. But in part, I became a vessel of guilt and badness in the marriage. These were feelings instilled in me from childhood. Whenever a problem arose, I believed it was always and only my fault. If someone was angry at me, I feared abandonment – I sometimes still do. After years in therapy, I learnt that my feelings were real, but not necessarily true; and it allowed me to tolerate my emotions and resist innate, automatic responses that included agreeing, apologizing, pleasing and placating. I didn't manage the issues constructively, so our bond weakened and finally broke down.

But relationships are the soil in which we learn and grow.

'Have your independence. Don't rush into anything. First settle yourself, and then get married,' Dad would say. He'd often reinforce (ad nauseum, actually) how important it was for us to become independent before getting involved romantically. Without realizing it, he was referencing the value of having a good sense of self – that clear and firm understanding of who you are – firstly, on your own, and then in relation to another person. I didn't fully appreciate his sentiment at the time.

Now I reflect and understand how I judged my parents and what was probably their life crises. I can see that they were just being normal young adults, who had gotten married way too young, and were just trying to figure out how to manage life, a young family, who they each were and their place in the world. Now I understand them and their 'mistakes' – many of which I've made too – and I don't judge. Nothing is ever perfect.

In later years, as my parents matured and resolved their personal dilemmas, their marriage became closer and loving. They were supportive and caring of each other, and although their squabbles continued to be a regular occurrence, they were each other's best friend and pillars of unwavering support.

Relationship breakdown is more the rule than the

exception these days. It's not surprising that many of my younger clients say that they would prefer never to get married, or that they would never bring children into the world. We have rightfully dissolved the idea of the fairytale prince and princess riding off into the sunset, but that doesn't mean it's impossible to have a functioning, healthy togetherness.

Because there are so many more options and variety, we do form connections differently these days. With dating sites and apps, we can pick and choose to our heart's content and swipe away at whatever doesn't seem to be for us. Despite the variety and accessibility of people to date, this is often a shallow exercise in human connection and gives a false expectation of finding 'the perfect one.' It can become tiring and confusing – both of which escalate feelings of apprehension and paranoia. But the spin-offs cannot be lumped into one basket. Both success and failure derive from this convenience, as the increased choice is simultaneously empowering and unfulfilling.

'I wish I'd known at your age what you already know,' I find myself saying to my young clients. Our children benefit from living in a psychologically minded society and are perhaps more astute in the realm of relationships than we ever were. Young clients remark that their worth doesn't derive from being valued by a partner, or that they are concerned about their partner's erratic emotions which portend disaster. They display heartening wisdom and insight into themselves and the interpersonal dynamics which will hopefully equip them for greater success.

But the downside to their greater knowledge and choice is perhaps the lack of resilience and persistence when things become more challenging.

I'm habitually asked, 'Do people change?' and 'What factors make for healthy and successful intimacy?' I dare not simplify a topic that has been so broadly researched and written about, but if forced to pick a single feature, I'd have to say it's having a partner who is willing to see themselves in the relationship equation and be as open to wanting to see your side too. Oh, communication and respect are part of that too.

Finding the right partner can be a tough journey. So much has to do with timing and each partner's sense of self-worth.

When seeking a partner, we may wonder, will I be good enough? When we are rejected, we tend to feel unworthy and *not* good enough; so it's important that we are comfortable with ourselves, knowing what we bring to the connection. We won't be for everyone. It has to be the right kind of healthy, balanced, respectful and loving partnership for us.

Not every day in a union is a happy one, but when two people mutually respect and care for each other and want the best for each other, kindness ensues. The strength of a healthy bond flows from our intentions and motivation.

I am grateful for Dad's messages of independence, self-belief, the value of experience and the importance of self-compassion.

Since my marriage ended, I've had the courage to take more chances, make new mistakes and learn from them. These days, I take responsibility for my growth and find myself in a more satisfying relationship – with myself. And others.

CHAPTER 25

Nurturing Our (Inner) Child

The school assembly hall was full to capacity as all students sat together on the left side of the room in their tidy rows of hard grey chairs. From the stage, it resembled a blue military – everyone was clothed in crisp, starched school dresses, shirts, ties and polished, reflective black shoes.

Prizegiving was my parents' favourite night of the year. As the Jewish outcasts in town, they revelled in the praise and admiration of others. On nights like these, they felt good enough – if not better – than everyone else.

The principal's voice bellowed over the microphone, 'The highest academic achievement in any grade goes to Lisa Myers.' Followed by loud applause, I made my way down the chair-lined walkway to the stairs at the bottom of the stage. The principal appeared dwarfed by the massive shiny trophy that donned my name twice before as I walked up the stairs to claim my prize. I had worked insanely hard for this brief moment. I needed to be the best at everything.

By this time, I was already used to working hard. I had started working at five years old by helping Dad in his fabric shop. My chest puffed out like a peacock's each time a customer commented, 'Wow, Sam, look at your daughter! She is so cute working here for you.' At twelve, I upskilled to waitressing, which brought in a reasonable income for years, including whilst I was studying medicine.

When people would ask, 'How do you manage it all, Lisa?' I'd become even more motivated to overcome my fatigue. Dad instilled the importance of a good work ethic, but he inadvertently also induced guilt and an overwhelming sense of responsibility for others in me. Consequently, I wasn't privy to the priceless art of moderation and how to separate my self-worth from my accomplishments. Dad hadn't wanted me to be the failure he perceived himself to be. Being the least successful of his brothers, who were all university graduates, Dad pushed and prized education – seeing it as the single route to success. Unknowingly, he would question my occasional poor results with hints of shame.

Dad did what he could to ensure I could study at university. He paid for my accommodation and provided me with a second-hand old red two-door Mazda that kept breaking down and wouldn't start in the winter because the freezing cold weather somehow affected the engine. It was so awful that once I earned a pay cheque, I bought myself a brand-new car.

'A new car is a waste,' Dad said, but I didn't care. I never wanted to be compromised ever again, stuck and unsafe on the side of the road. Since then, I only buy new yet inexpensive cars, no doubt the impact of my past imprinting.

I loved the adoration my achievements brought me, as did my parents. But more than that, I loved making them happy, particularly Dad. It seemed to be my job.

This 'job' has been passed down to my daughter, Daniella. I hear myself echoed when she says, 'I hate that you aren't happy and I'm disappointing you,' if she perceives she's not meeting my expectations. As a parent, I try to separate what my girls do from who they are even though my feedback doesn't always support this. I reinforce that 'what you do is not who you are,' in the hope that with age and understanding, they will know this, if not emotionally, then at least, cognitively.

Essentially, all I want is for my children to be happy with who they are, to become good humans who are kind, considerate and respectful of themselves and others. But I also want them to comprehend that they have to work hard to achieve their goals, whatever those may be. I know that life is tough, so my role is to ensure their resilience, self-belief and the ability to problem-solve when things don't go to plan.

The truth is, it has taken time for me to accept and become comfortable with my children's achievements – not due to any fault of theirs. I have had to learn that my job is to bring out their best by encouraging them as I steer, support and love them for who they are and not what they do or what I believe is good for them. As parents, we can only compare our children to the previous day's version of themselves, knowing that they will get to where they need to go, given enough time, help and love.

In the past, when my children have been struggling, I've had sleepless nights obsessively checking their phones and drawers for journals to discern information to help me understand what is really going on so I can 'fix' their lives. I've badgered them to open up to me because 'I do this job and other people pay for my advice.' But this is not healthy parenting behaviour. I've over-identified with my own childhood feelings of being left out and not enough. I've had to learn that my feelings aren't my children's, and that my job is not only to teach them but also to slow down and separate enough to learn from their valuable lessons.

But I've frequently let my feelings get in the way of best supporting my children. I once felt hurt, and as if I had personally failed, when Daniella didn't get a place at a dance recital. I justified all the reasons she shouldn't feel bad, assuming she must be feeling as miserable as I was. I couldn't tolerate her imagined heartbreak (which was really just my own, or a sense of failure I'd passed on to her) and wanted to alleviate it immediately, despite knowing that developing the emotional muscle to overcome these moments of disappointment will only accelerate her growth and ability to cope with future disappointments.

I've let both children's academic ability, drive and ambition cause me stress. When Daniella was in year K, after flashing cards with sight words to her and her friends, I panicked because she wasn't firing out the words like her peers. I immediately arranged for an IQ assessment, worried that she had learning difficulties, only to discover she was completely within the range of 'normal.' Because I'd worked obsessively through school and university, and have extreme expectations of myself, I'd lost the ability to discern what is normal and good enough. The results helped relieve my fears, guide my expectations and let me identify the areas in which she needed help. It took me time to learn that my children are happy and don't need or want the same things as I did at school. They are on their own journeys to discover who they are.

I'm often stunned by their creativity and ability to celebrate rather than compete with their peers' successes. I've watched their growing perspective on the value of hard work and effort as opposed to agitating about their achievements. I was the one who ill-tolerated being average and feeling useless, heavily driven by my parents' sentiments. I never wanted to be 'that parent' who only perceives their child as a narcissistic extension of themselves and is ashamed by their lack of success. Those generational wheels didn't need to keep turning.

My girls are different from me and from one another. It's been both a painful and rewarding journey as I learn to embrace their unique strengths and qualities, and make sure they feel it and not only hear it. I have to keep monitoring myself and not reacting to the feelings triggered by my childhood trauma that come up in me.

I love and admire my girls' personalities, their quirkiness, vivid imaginations and deep intuition and sensitivity, but am cautious writing about them, knowing they have their own paths. I can't use them to deal with my issues as my parents did to me.

Parents question and worry constantly about their children.

Have I done the right thing, said the wrong thing, ruined

them for life? Will they be okay? Will they have friends, a future, a job? Will this be a problem forever?

Not only have I heard these questions from clients, I have also voiced them myself.

I am often put on the spot when it comes to my parenting as people regard me as the 'expert.' Raising two teenage girls has been interesting, challenging, stressful and painful. When she reached the teen years, Daniella pulled away from me once again; but this time, I found it easier to handle, knowing her anger and resentment was normal teen behaviour. And if I just gave her enough space, time and boundaries, it would subside. It did. Somehow, I find it more difficult to let go of my younger one. I have to resist the urge to mother her in the ways *I* need to feel useful and, in the process, inadvertently stifle her normal developmental process of individuation.

Some teens behave archetypically and respond well to having clear communication and a gradual increase in independence in proportion to their growing sense of responsibility. I was like this as a teenager. Ideally, we want our teens to feel safe enough to be open with us as their parents.

But some don't fit this stereotype. Every child is different – neither good nor bad. Some need more protecting from their peers and support for their social challenges. At the same time, we have to be careful not to make them feel worse and as if they are the problem.

My daughter Rachel often says, 'Mum, you can't see everything I do as part of the same problem or thing!'

If we ask too many questions and make too many suggestions about how to fit in, we may suffocate and stifle our kids. They may end up avoiding us to protect their self-worth. Our job as parents is to manage our past traumas and shames so we don't feel hurt or annoyed that our teens don't fit in.

As an adolescent, I did everything to fit in. I'd grown up in an Afrikaans-dominated town in South Africa, and my friends were all Christian. I was so desperate to be part of their group that one day, I decided to give up my Jewish faith and adopt theirs. I asked one of my girlfriend's mothers to help me with the transition because she was the most religious and connected to God. I sat on her bed, and she placed her hands on my shoulders, then prayed for Jesus to accept me as his child.

Following that, I once snuck out of home to attend a Sunday church service. When my parents found out, I was surprised at how calm and understanding my father was – though Mum was not. Dad explained that he'd experienced similar feelings growing up without many Jewish friends. I was shocked, never having thought my parents could ever understand my challenges. But they did and even had helpful advice, the kind that radiates from the perspective of age and experience.

It's difficult when life doesn't simply flow, and what seems so easy for other parents and their children eludes your own family. You might find yourself angry at the apparent unfairness of the situation, the lack of support and compassion. It can be very isolating.

Teenagers don't need us to reinforce their already heightened feelings of being different. They need us to see their beautiful qualities and admire their strength of character. All it takes is for us to imagine and empathise with how tough it is to be a teenager these days.

Our role is to be an advocate for them and to educate those who fail to tolerate difference. If we are struggling, it's a sign that we have more work to do on ourselves in letting go, stepping back and offering our kids the time to grow and develop maturity. They need to feel that we have confidence in them, that our love for them is unbiased so they can seek us, step closer and hear our wisdom; and we can hear theirs.

We can't erase past errors, but it's never too late to learn and grow. Our teenagers need our unconditional acceptance. Sometimes, in trying to help, we only reinforce the idea that our child is a problem or has one. They are not assisted by us finding fault with them. When we accept them in this way, we open ourselves to finding other supportive, understanding and non-judgemental parents who are going through similar challenges with their teens. Our children's innate traits aren't their behaviours. We are called to love their uniqueness, and to set limits on their actions.

Even with all my training and understanding, I still fret, ruminate and feel sad every time I witness one of my children hurting. We may think we know how to help our kids; but they may refuse our help, leaving us powerless to deal with our own emotions. As the adults, we are the ones who must discern the fine line between pushing them out of their comfort zone and celebrating their station in life. It requires careful and constant monitoring of our own feelings and motivations.

We have to let go of trying to 'fix' our kids (which only makes them feel broken) and avoid over-identifying with their pain. Our energy is best invested in co-building bridges to overcome their hitches, rather than attacking or defending them. We have to become their constant, neutral container, holding all and offering little more than a gentle nudge and untold support. Anything too direct can feel overly scrutinising and can expand the wedge between us and them.

My own experiences enrich my compassion for parents who come seeking my professional guidance. Together, we share the authenticity of our struggles and become companions on the parenting path.

My dad raised me to feel I was capable of achieving whatever I set my mind to. I only hope to do the same for my children. Like any parent, I've experienced twists, turns, tears and laughs in raising my daughters – and I'm sure there will be many more to come. I'm getting better at it; but I still sometimes feel anger, frustration, loss and sadness when I witness their struggles and wish I could take their pain away even though I know I can't.

That's when I remind myself that resilience grows fastest watered by life not going to plan.

CHAPTER 26

The Mirror of Self-Reflection

My very first panic attack happened on a Wednesday at 6pm. I remember these details because anxiety leaves its mark on you indelibly.

I was newly engaged to Steven and had started my very first registrar job at the Helen Joseph Hospital in Johannesburg. Helen Joseph was a British-born political activist in South African politics and years after her death was honoured with the ANC's highest award for devotion to the liberation struggle. I liked the idea of starting my career at a hospital named after a strong woman with such a powerful cause – to free people from the hell of suffering.

I lived a thirty-minute drive from the hospital. Being called out at night was scary, and I'd pray from the moment I'd start the car's ignition until I gratefully returned home, never having stopped at a red traffic light on the crime-ridden streets. I was always hyper-aroused and anxious about my safety because a colleague had been shot in the leg driving out the main gates of Baragwanath, the largest hospital in the southern hemisphere in the township of Soweto.

On this particular night, I'd been called to the emergency department after a horrifically stressful day. My parents had sent Ralph up to Johannesburg to live with me for a while after his recent divorce. He was vulnerable and struggling to pick up the fragments of his life, and I'd spent the day caring for him. This was my role in the family as rescuer – I'd always looked after him, dating back to his first days at school when I was summoned by my parents to manage his separation anxiety and accompany him into the classroom.

In the wake of his marriage ending, I was helping him to find a job, giving him a temporary home and carrying him through his day-to-day as he made his way back to full strength. I would drill him with positive psychology statements such as, 'You can do it!' and 'You will get through this!'

Over the years, I'd provided ongoing moral support and instinctively knew how to go through the motions of uplifting those struggling around me. Truthfully, I didn't really know whether it would *actually* be okay. The reality is that I *never* truly know, but I've trained my mind to refuse the alternative. For a long time, I was a victim, believing that I had no sources of help and in the process, undermined the support that was there. But I have since learnt to overcome my shame when I need others, and if I need assistance, I take responsibility for reaching out. Sometimes, help won't be readily available, but even that realisation can be beneficial. I always try to keep perspective when others don't seem to be there when I need them, as I know everyone has their own life and challenges.

My brother's tension caused him to suffer from cluster headaches. On this particular day, when I was on call for emergency at the hospital, I also had to squeeze in a doctor's visit with him, which had escalated my stress. Flustered, I responded to the phone call notifying me of a psychotic patient in the Emergency Department. I then rushed to The Helen Joseph with the radio playing in the background. At some point on that drive, an extreme fear overcame me. It seemed as if the radio was speaking to me.

I'd already started my psychiatry training and had dealt with clients with psychotic disorders like schizophrenia. In this moment, I suddenly panicked that I was having a hallucination or a referential delusion. I'd heard about these from clients – was that now happening to me? I immediately switched off the radio. I don't know how but, in this state, I arrived at the hospital, attended to the patient and then drove home, distressed.

Later, I shared this experience with a colleague who suggested I'd had a psychotic or micro-psychotic episode – perhaps he thought the word *micro* would reduce my edginess. It did not. I discussed it with a more senior specialist in psychiatry who explained that I'd had an anxiety attack. He suggested I talk to a psychologist.

I was relieved.

I immediately booked to see a therapist. I continued with therapy fairly consistently until the year before Dad died. By then, I felt comfortable, stable and was able independently to manage the frequent ups and downs of life, implementing the knowledge and strategies I'd learned over the years.

But after Dad died, I went back to therapy.

Anxiety can paralyse the strongest among us, making the simplest tasks appear impossible. Generally, our anxiety signals a deeper inner conflict that needs resolution.

When I was six years old, I wrote this in a local newspaper. M*y name is Lisa and I am six years old. I have dark curly hair, and when I grow up, I want to be a doctor.*

My aspiration was always to help others, but my need was to rescue, as I was petrified of the world crumbling around me. Therapy guided my journey and helped me recognise that my mind made my thoughts bigger than the reality.

I was stronger than I believed I was. Others coped fine without me. I was afraid of being abandoned. I could set boundaries, avoid enabling helplessness, entreaty help and know that I wasn't inferior or being taxing on others.

But I have always felt an overwhelming duty towards my family – I recognise this with hindsight. I now occasionally repeat this pattern when I expect my older daughter to care for her younger sibling. This isn't necessarily 'wrong,' but when done in extremes, can cause overt, unnecessary obligatory guilt and burdens the one left with the responsibility. Even the most independent children deeply need love and support despite their appearances of capability. We can help them to shirk the burden of always accommodating others' needs and wants by occasionally facilitating and tolerating their unravelling.

A good, safe therapy space can feel like home,

and for me, it allowed me to repeat the journey from childhood to adulthood. I learnt who I was and could muster compassion for my younger version or inner child. By internalising my therapist's voice, I could germinate and grow mine, enough to win a fruitful debate with my negative inner critic.

I'd grown up having parents with good intentions. But the limitations of their knowledge made them, at times, unintentionally inconsistent, avoidant, shaming, critical, uncontained or reversed in roles. My parents were authoritative and demanded respect. I became more resilient while burying my anxiety; but in children less capable and confident, this dynamic can aggravate their anxiety and make them emotionally chaotic, clingy, attention-seeking, fragmented and disorganised.

Children not securely bonded to parents who can help them contain their emotions sometimes cope by being extremely rigid and controlled or at the other extreme of the spectrum, become desperately clingy and ramp up the expression of their emotions to elicit care.

I didn't always feel safe around Mum's anger. My parents' default was to place blame, so I believed I was the problem. Many times, the unconscious repetition of our parent-child dynamic would cast me in the role of that horrible person; and by acting out spitefully, I'd only give them more ammunition to use against me. Little did I realise that projections between us evoked my horrible and nasty side. It made me prove them right repeatedly because I couldn't possibly believe that I was good inside when I was given all their badness to hold and made to acknowledge my own. This became my pattern to repair in later relationships.

Today, many parents want to rectify the mistakes of their parents, and end up over-identifying with their children in the sort of situations that affected them most during childhood – the ones they vowed never to repeat. Old-school, dictatorial and distant parenting has evolved New Age parents, better at connecting to their child's feelings, but perhaps, not adequately developed in managing them. When parents are able to effectively contain their feelings, they avoid the massive overspill from either parent and child, which creates secondary calamitous ramifications.

Helicopter parenting, or over-involved parenting, may be the knee-jerk overcompensation for growing up with minimal parental involvement. It could be a response to anxiety or the desire for perfection. But no matter the cause, it overshadows and denies a child's autonomous development.

So is there a right way to parent, and is it possible to be a 'good parent' when we haven't had an adequate example to follow? Can we re-parent ourselves and rectify past dysfunction? We can, actually. This is where we learn to embrace the concept of a 'good enough' parent. To be 'good enough' is to be self-aware, capable of offering containment, able to manage our own emotions and provide strong, clear and safe boundaries and be a model of self-regulation to our children.

I have found therapy to be a valuable reparenting process in which I have learned to manage my life and separate what is controllable and what isn't. I have been empowered by knowledge which has taught me to challenge my automatic feelings and thoughts, and not let them solidify into simple truths. I can interject my pattern repetition and steer away from derailing, self-sabotaging, automatic responses that no longer serve my adult self. I've realised that many of the behaviours I used in my childhood to ensure safety and connection, like pleasing or being perfect, are no longer appropriate or necessary. I can correct any beliefs generated by past life experiences, knowing how these sift reality, impacting my view on life, people in it and myself.

When I find myself blaming other people, it is a cue to me. I immediately recognise that I need to engage in deeper self-exploration and take responsibility for my role in the dynamic. It's more difficult when I am emotional as my filters are weaker, and past truths become overpowering monsters.

Behaviours stem from thoughts and feelings. So as we walk similar known paths, even if they are uncomfortable, we cement our dysfunction. When we lack consciousness of our role, we imagine disaster is just bad luck, and we take no responsibility for the situations that arise in our lives. Or we become the victim and bemoan that others have it easier. Without self-awareness, we lose the opportunity to reflect and change.

I've heard people deride therapy for all kinds of reasons, including that it just allows us to blame others for our problems. This is untrue. Good therapy involves grieving ideal love, expressing anger and frustration in a healthy way, processing pain, taking responsibility and ultimately, integrating experiences to create a more consolidated narrative of life. Firstly, you have to see, then you can let go; and finally, take steps forward. There are many layers to the process which requires persistence, consistency and patience.

People may call it psychiatry, but I call it life – the practice of learning to manage and cope in the best, most flexible manner possible. It is something we all have to do.

Who knows what the role of synchronicity and coincidence is in our lives? I believe that the presence of my colleague in South Africa when I experienced my first panic attack – a critical sliding door moment in my life – was a conduit in my journey to become a psychiatrist.

When I had that panic attack, I wasn't psychotic rather, merely anxious. But it's a feeling that can cause the strongest of us to spin wildly out of control. It can manifest in a multitude of ways, instigating physical, emotional and cognitive symptoms. It's not uncommon during a moment of panic for people to believe they are having a heart attack or going crazy because you feel as if you're losing touch with reality. This is exactly what happened to me. Many people are astounded to discover that what they perceived as a life-threatening illness was, in fact, simply a panic attack.

In all moments of darkness, we can find the light of meaning.

Looking back, I can see how that feeling of panic connected me to the power of therapy. That, in turn, has let me rewire my brain, reshape my mind and change my life. For all these gifts, I am grateful.

CHAPTER 27

Walking at Someone Else's Pace

Sharing a client's journey has to be one of the most rewarding aspects of my job. It's a privilege that I never take for granted. As a companion in another person's voyage of self-discovery, I don't have the right to push or decide which direction they should go. My role is to be a guide and shed light on their blind spots, which we all have.

If a client isn't ready to engage, I feel it unethical to stir up their emotions, when they may not be supported once they leave my rooms. Although I encourage my clients' decisions and autonomy, it worries and saddens me that they might struggle alone and beyond what is necessary without the invaluable reassurance of a gentle helping hand. I felt that strongly with one of my clients, Matt.

Matt sat sullenly across from me. He was a lovely, kind and caring young man, who was also very highly strung. He discussed an incident that had occurred with his older sister, Ally, whom I knew was also stressed, but better at hiding it than her brother.

A dejected looking Matt spoke, 'Ally was really frustrated when she looked at me and asked why I'm always so stressed. Then she let out a massive sigh, as if I was draining her with my negative energy.'

He turned his question to me. 'Is that how I am seen? I feel terrible because it's not who I want to be.'

'Who do you want to be?' I asked.

'I want to be relaxed and well rounded,' he confessed. He was devastated that his ideal version of himself was a hundred and eighty degrees in contrast to how others perceived him.

'Ally massaged my shoulders to ease my tension and asked me whether I was happy.'

Matt explained that he wasn't confident responding to his sister, knowing how he hated the fact he found it impossible to feel happiness or be happy. 'I try so hard to be happy, but it's difficult for me. Everyone says I should just let it in, and I'm not really sure what that means.'

I thought about how important it was for his healing to let his sadness in.

Matt had grown up with a narcissistic, angry, abusive and manipulative father who had scared Matt and worse, made him feel small and shameful. Matt, like many children who know no different, tried to escape the pain of his shame by moulding himself into someone representing excellence. He wanted to be seen as perfect, calm, together and capable – never stressed, anxious, uncontrolled or weak.

At the end of high school, he moved overseas and found himself in an awful situation. He lived in a cheap room with a family whose mother was very ill. Matt felt compelled to care for the mother, despite being totally unprepared and ill-equipped. He was inexpert at saying no, not wanting to let anyone down. He didn't want to appear entitled or spoilt, self-views that had been instilled by his own father, who had always projected his personal feelings of badness and worthlessness onto those around him to maintain his sense of grandiosity and righteousness. Matt found himself far from home, isolated, inexperienced and lonely. He felt trapped and afraid, and consequently froze, doing everything and anything he was told, like a Cinderella. Matt was expected to cook, clean and nurse his overseas family every day.

Then one night, he was assaulted by an older woman who was visiting her unwell relative. Matt felt a mixture of lust and arousal as well as shame, disgust and guilt. In our sessions, he described how he had never shared these experiences due to embarrassment and feelings of being tarnished and dirty. He knew that society would high five him for 'getting with an older woman,' but he longed to rid his life of these experiences and his mind of the memories.

Matt's life-long heavy burden of defectiveness, disgrace and blame had made him strive to be a textbook child and young adult. He denied all the ugly parts of his personality and the imperfect moments in his life to function and have control. After leaving the structured school environment where Matt was highly regarded for his star-kid status, he found himself lost, confused and riddled with failure, angst and misery.

Until he came to see me, Matt had never processed

his trauma, felt the range of his emotions, recognised all faces of his character or accepted himself. As a result, he was stuck. His words and ways were all too familiar, and they echoed my earlier shame-ridden years of striving for ultimate control and perfection. I too had done everything to prevent the ugly and embarrassing shadows from casting darkness over my glistening exterior.

In our sessions, I focused on helping him to share and articulate his story so he could off-load his feelings of dishonour and inadequacy, and forgive himself for being human. Over time, Matt was able to confront the terror of being found out for being blemished and just normal. Our time together gave him the opportunity to express his undesirable emotions and experience being held without judgement, which allowed him to tolerate his pain until it subsided. He re-learnt self-trust, how to set boundaries and how to avoid the influence and impact of others' opinions, particularly his older siblings whom he'd always regarded as flawless. I related keenly with his need to impress and gain approval. Matt acquainted himself with his sadness, began to treat it tenderly and provided it with sufficient breathing room instead of always forcing himself to be joyful.

About a year had passed, when towards the end of our usual fortnightly catchup, Matt said, 'Lisa, I think I am okay and would prefer to reach out when I need you rather than having set times to talk. I always feel the need to prepare for our sessions.'

He had not entirely learnt to rely on his instinct, be himself and let go of his concerns about being evaluated by another person. But still, he had come far and was ready to move onto the next chapter of his life. Although, I had a sense of his path ahead and the areas in which he still needed to grow, I knew he needed my belief in him, not my opinions. Ironically, the scheduled sessions were supposed to be an opportunity for him to forego his need to impress and please, but I could acknowledge that forcing Matt to engage in *my* plan for him would only replicate the role he was forced to play by his family and those who had dictated how he should live his life.

I got a little teary as we concluded our final session. It was an ending, and those always evoke feelings of loss and sadness in me. I felt anxious letting him go, knowing that he struggled with his low moods as he chased the elation of his accomplishments. But it wasn't necessary to share my thoughts with Matt.

Instead, I offered, 'I am proud of you and the time you have taken to work on the many aspects of your life. Please remember, being down is normal, and don't let yourself believe you are a failure when failure happens to you. Be kind to yourself at those times. Let it settle and remind yourself how far you have come. It will pass, and when it does, you can reflect and truly enjoy the good moments.'

Losing Dad has taught me that we can never take on another person's journey. Sometimes, we have to respect that people will make choices we wouldn't choose for them, and that is okay.

CHAPTER 28

Triggered by Our Every Day

'My daughter is having her baby in a week. I know I should be excited, but all I can think about is the baby I lost,' Sarissa said.

Over the screen, in our telehealth consultation, I watched her wrap her arms around herself and pat her shoulders in a self-soothing gesture to calm her inner child. She closed her eyes. 'It will be okay,' she said to herself. 'I do this, and it helps.'

I had been working with Sarissa for a while now to help her deal with her history of abuse.

'Isn't it amazing how an event in someone else's life can affect us so much?' Not only was the upcoming birth of her grandchild evoking the grief of losing an unborn child decades back, but it was also bringing up all her own childhood trauma of abuse and neglect, which was even further back in her past.

Sarissa acknowledged the duality of her responses. She felt both elated at the prospect of becoming a grandmother as well as guilt because it was also triggering the resurgence of her past traumas. She was experiencing vicarious trauma, which is the 'second-hand' trauma and associated symptoms we experience when we witness and hear others' experiences – even positive ones – that retrigger our own negative associations. Sitting with Sarissa, I noted the inner whispers of my own past horrors and made a mental note of trauma's snowball effect.

'I can't sleep. I'm waking up in the middle of the night and can't get back to sleep. I have terrible diarrhoea, and my heart and mind are racing. I know it's stress, and I'm trying to be kind to myself and set boundaries where I can.'

Her niece was supposed to visit, and usually, she would have offered her a room; but Sarissa had let her know that because she was struggling, it wasn't the best time for visitors. Many people suffering from poor mental health find it difficult to let people close to them know what is happening, but as Sarissa had come to understand her trauma, she had developed effective skills to manage her life. She compromised and offered to pick her niece up and take her to dinner. Even though her fear came up frequently, she had learnt not to engage it. She knew it was just her body reacting and had become adept at simply breathing into it.

Initially, she'd dealt with it as many of us do – by 'splitting off' various 'parts' of herself, each representing a different chronological developmental life stage. There was the fearful child; the angry, impulsive adolescent; the needy young woman desperate for male validation; and her older, wiser self which often had to step in and re-parent the 'children' within her. Over time, she had acquired a healthier repertoire of coping skills which included strategies such as self-expansion, remaining grounded and simply observing her nagging negative thoughts about past traumatic events without judgement. She would repeat the mantra, 'Let be and embrace,' which allowed her to tolerate the unwanted parts of her life. Now she had accumulated a mental and emotional armoury of self-soothing, mindfulness, compassion and acceptance practices.

In moments like these, I am overcome with awe at the courage of my clients. These small steps may not seem like much, but they are the difference between coping and falling apart.

Many of my clients have learned these competences, which they adapt to their own afflictions and personalities. One addresses her negative thoughts as companions for the day. She says, 'Okay, thoughts, you and I are going to have to be together today. Come along then. That way, I needn't fight and try resist them.'

In Sarissa's case, the upcoming birth of her grandchild had sparked her multiple, terrifying, marring childhood experiences. Her own inner child was panicked, yet frozen and numb, detached from all emotion and reality. She explained how she hadn't always been able to identify her triggers. 'At times, there is no reason, and it's so scary.'

She was not to know how deeply I resonated with her paralysis. For weeks, I'd been unable to write this book while I was dealing with the fallout of my own vicarious trauma. It had been innocently triggered by a Facebook post by my writing mentor.

As I read her words, my heart stopped. I knew she had left her life and family in Sydney to go spend time with her sick mother while she was having chemotherapy back in Africa. But while she was there, her mother had died unexpectedly. In sharing her grief, she had posted an image of Smudge, her mother's cat sitting on her bed and the words, 'Mommy isn't coming back Smudge.' The sadness trickled down my cheeks as I thought how difficult loss is for those left behind, creating an unfillable void. I snuggled my dog, Harley, and felt soothed by her soft, fluffy coat. My heart ached, contemplating losing her or her, me. For months, I had spoken to my mentor in depth about my grief, but now it was her chapter to pen. Despite our professional connection, the vicarious nature of trauma and loss evoked a frozen storm within, and I stumbled.

Our regular mentoring session was understandably cancelled, whilst she attended her mother's funeral and sat *shiva*. Her loss became a grief-a-deux, and my writing stopped. I felt sad and didn't want to think about my dad. I was surprisingly completely stuck. I had been flung from the logical lobes of my left brain, into the emotive pathways of my right. I felt desolate, numb and empty, yet at the same time, bounding with emotion.

Once again, I was stuck, trapped in my grief-cave. Everyone's trauma felt magnified. I avoided my feelings and thoughts about Dad that had resurfaced and was flung back into doing bite-size, 'automated' tasks as I distracted myself, patiently waiting for the trauma tornado to pass.

Trauma shuts the gate around our minds. It raises the

bridge that ties us to life and those around us, creating a sense of isolation and immobilisation. Like a sleep paralysis, we are awake and aware, yet can't move or scream for help, as if dead in a living body. These common and horrific trauma manifestations make us feel detached from reality (dissociation), that we ourselves are unreal (depersonalisation) and that the world around us is unreal (derealisation). We may feel out of body, observing ourselves from above and living in a world that seems like a movie or a dream. We dissociate when facing our feelings because they are petrifying. When physically fleeing is impossible, we opt to escape mentally and float away. The experience is frequently more disturbing than the initial trigger, and we are trapped.

This is one of the reasons why some trauma victims self-harm. It's their way of grounding themselves and bringing them back to reality so that they feel something rather than numb. Or it may rid and release their overwhelming pain and terror. The visceral pain frequently validates their unseen suffering.

I don't want to minimise, exclude or disrespect any person by simplifying the complexity of managing the aftermath of trauma. As a professional, I advocate for a slow, stepwise approach to processing trauma and having a contained, supportive space in which to do it. In the first stages following a trauma, you feel confused, pained, terrified and shameful. It is understandable when we default into denial; but if we are to heal, we have to expose, process and integrate. This requires patience, tenderness and a flexible, sometimes tailored, approach. I've found writing healing. By constructing a narrative, I have had gentle re-exposure, allowing sufficient time to process my trauma and desensitise to the intensity of my emotions.

Sufferers often avoid acknowledging their emotions, fearing it will facilitate further problems, cause additional pain, burden others and will be seen as indulging personal hardship. On the contrary, understanding our trauma provides a scaffolding on which to build self-compassion and enhanced resilience. Denial never rids us of an experience. It sets the timer on an uncontrollable, ticking landmine – one wrong move and *boom!* Letting your heart drip like a leaking tap, slowly emitting the hurt, gives you time to process and familiarise your thoughts and feelings, gaining relief and the empowerment of understanding.

'It's okay to compartmentalise,' I soothed a friend who was sorrowful after having to watch her father's consecration over a Zoom call the previous day. COVID-19 had banned her from travelling to America to attend the commemoration in person. She was understandably heavy hearted.

I explained my coping mechanism, and how I deal with the fluctuating, intense emotions that are tied to my grief: 'It's sometimes so hard to feel and still live your daily life. Sometimes, I push it aside because it's too much to think about, and I have to concentrate on work or the children. I don't have the capacity to cope with all of it and don't feel strong enough to go there.'

'Thank you,' she said. 'I felt so bad not always thinking about him. As if I were betraying him, or somehow not showing my deep love or my heartbreaking pain.'

Giving myself time to grieve at any time – because

grief doesn't follow normal time frames – has been my only way of coping.

It took six weeks after I read my mentor's Facebook post that I found myself back at my writing. My fingers typed away. I'd taken a first step and felt overjoyed. The ensnaring strings of sorrow had loosened, leaving me free to move again.

Understanding my own fluctuating grief gives me the chance to open my heart when a new grief script arrives in the form of a client.

CHAPTER 29

A Goodbye Needs No Script

Every story of loss is unique and varies in intensity. But some losses are more complicated than others. 'Complicated grief' is a term used to describe prolonged, intense grief which lasts more than six months or in which the griever becomes completely preoccupied with the deceased. As a result, the grief begins to have a negative impact on the mourner's ability to function in their everyday life.

I'm wary of the use of the word *complicated*, which feels synonymous with any grieving process. Yet some circumstances trouble the loss more deeply than others. This was the case with my client, Charlie. He had found his younger brother lifeless on his bed and had tried unsuccessfully to save his life. Sometimes, the facts I hear in a day's work can shatter your heart.

'I should have been the one to die,' he said as he sat sullenly and expressionless in the chair opposite me. His head was bowed, and his lanky body hunched with arms dangling alongside his oversized feet. His height made his posture awkward, as if he didn't know how to fit inside his own skin.

'I called for my dad,' he continued. 'He came. We tried. He was crying, screaming.' Charlie's voice was staccato-like. He avoided my eyes as he continued. 'Our lives were bad before, but now, it's worse. At least he made them happy. I don't. It should have been me.'

Charlie's painful words are not uncommon in people who are left behind. What he was expressing is typical survivor guilt, the feeling of not deserving to live when others haven't been as fortunate. When Charlie's parents later joined us in the session, I anticipated they would share the events surrounding their son's awful death. Instead, they only spoke about their difficulties in parenting Charlie. Sometimes, what we most need to talk about becomes the hardest thing to broach. We call this avoidance, and it is partially adaptive, meaning how people adapt or cope with shock and pain. But as I listened, I felt it verged on the maladaptive – where a coping strategy becomes destructive.

In Charlies' family's case, the conflict seemed to obliterate their loss. They danced around the grief like a raging fire that risked burning them, but their clashing only stoked the flames and created further distance amongst them. My job was to help them understand that though they could not save their deceased son's life, but they could fix the turmoil of their relationship. Side-stepping their failure was only going to create further catastrophe. Unfortunately, they weren't ready to address their grief and remained trapped in their web of struggle. All I could do was simply offer considered reflections of my observations and express my ongoing availability if ever they wished to engage with their grief.

It's common in the early stages of a traumatic loss to avoid the elephant of grief in the room; but unprocessed loss festers and can lead to complicated and prolonged grief marked by depression, addictions, relationship breakdown, life dysfunction and despair. Fear of further loss might cause us to cling tightly to those left behind. This explains Charlie's parents' escalated protectiveness and preoccupation with him. He, on the other hand, pushed back and experienced it as invasive and unnecessary.

Each of us has to process grief for the sake of closure, which is a form of tolerance more than it is acceptance. Even if we don't accept our loss, we have to learn to live with it.

When people get sick before they die, we might have the opportunity to begin grieving sooner. Time with a dying loved one gives us space for comprehensive farewells, forgiveness, repair and mastery over the processes we can't control. When we feel helpful, it alleviates our powerlessness in being unable to fix or change their unspeakable circumstances.

When illness and imminent death turns a loved one into a stranger or fragment of the person we knew, we have to process these confronting moments. If we are separated from them in their final days (now more so due to COVID-19) and have to farewell them over a video or phone call or not at all, feelings of destitution, regret, remorse and extra heartache are added to the mix.

Sudden loss means you start mourning when the

person dies. I didn't have the opportunity to farewell Dad and regret not having spoken to him frequently in the weeks and months prior to his death, which left our differences unresolved. At the very least, I wish I could have told him one last time that I loved him. As well as absorbing the shock of the loss, we are also left with many unanswered questions. In my case, I regret not demanding a comprehensive autopsy to determine the events surrounding Dad's death, which might have alleviated my ongoing vivid imaginings of his horrible pain. This is one of the issues I will have to deal with in my grief journey forever.

I began journaling to process my thoughts and emotions after Dad died and found writing helpful in organizing my feelings. I advocate it for clients who need to do the same. It allows me to reflect on my progress. Initially, I used it to express raw emotion; but over time, it has evolved into considered reflections that are slightly more removed from my core pain. I miss the constant intensity of those early entries because it connected me to Dad; but in that space, I couldn't function, be there for my children or do my work with the depth it needs.

My final communications with Dad were messages on social media posts that he would never read. I have continued my relationship with him through the writing of this book, and keep it alive when I talk about him in conversation and connect with him whilst meditating. I always visualise him at the end of a tunnel that radiates a bright light. Every action I take to this end, relieves me.

I value the time I now have with Mum even if it could be more frequent – but I forgive myself for only being human.

It's unreal and impossible to live life as if every day might be the last. It negates the normalcy of expressing a full and broad range of emotions in our relationships.

Achieving closure is an essential component of mourning, and there is no single right way. It is an infinite process, and to progress might include circulating, undulating or reversing as the many emotions find their resting place. It asks of us kindness and tolerance of our humanness. When clients voice feeling guilty for what they have said or failed to voice to someone they've lost, I remind them that a 'bad' person wouldn't be bothered by these 'mistakes.'

The finality of death challenges our human need to know and control our lives.

Mourning should not be glamorised or forced. For some of us, death may bring retribution or relief if we have lived for years with hurt and pain caused by the departed person. There is no rule that we *have* to make amends, ask forgiveness, love, long for or show respect. Everyone's grief is personal.

Since losing Dad, my interest in hearing other stories of loss has grown. It's helped me to speak about my grief, so it felt natural to provide those who wanted to share their unique stories and intimate memories of lost loved ones the same opportunity. It's brought me joy to see their eyes light up in remembrance, and we are consoled in our mutual understanding.

It commonly takes a certain amount of time for mourners to make sense of what is senseless, surreal or incredibly sad. Some find the grieving process an opportunity to heal relationships that have been rife with upset and anger, as was the case with my friend Garth.

'My father wasn't always a good man, and he put us through hell. The last days I spent with him were about forgiveness and seeking peace with it all,' he told me, sharing how he spent two-hundred-and-fifty-seven days and six hours, five minutes and three seconds sitting with his sick father every day. During this time, he processed all the moments of hurt his father had caused people over his lifetime, including him. Although his father wasn't religious, Garth felt it important to pray and repent on behalf of his father. My friend needed to gain mastery over what had been out of his control for many years, and grieving gave him this opportunity.

'My dad always gave us a hard time about money and once threatened to end his life in front of us because of money. It was a very tough upbringing. He didn't know better, but he was terrible to us and everyone else, completely absorbed in himself.'

I asked him how he felt after his father had passed on.

'Fine,' he replied. Then added, 'I miss my dad though. But I said everything I needed to say to him and have no regrets. I made amends with the hurt he caused. The time we spent together allowed me to understand and forgive him. He was so fragile at the end, physically, but I could see his emotional fragility and how fear had made him an asshole because he tried to ignore that smallness he felt.'

He explained how his father had always made him feel inferior, but helping him through his dying made Garth realise that his father had made him a better and stronger human. His father was forced to confront the damage he had caused and how guilty he'd made Garth feel. Garth had always imagined money as the be-all to life. But since his father's death, he has been able to let go of these ideas.

There is no script for how we each make peace. I've had to find solace too in the shards of my father's death. Despite no formal goodbye, my father knew I loved him. We always shared a special bond. Dad told Mum I would care for her, and he gave me the opportunity to continue repairing any feelings of not having done my share.

This book is part of my goodbye. Every page is inspired by his life, our relationship and his legacy as he would have wanted – in helping other people.

CHAPTER 30

The Spectrum of Trauma

After Dad died, my thoughts and emotions were so scattered that it was near impossible to fathom whether I was in the present or the past. It felt confusing, as though my brain was strewn with thoughts. My sleep became fractured and nightmares, the norm. I recognised these as symptoms of PTSD.

I had heard it all before from clients – the shadows out of the corner of your eye, startling at everything and anything, the triggers inducing anxiety and fear, images flashing in front of your eyes – but now, I was experiencing it all firsthand. Sometimes, I was intrigued at being personally immersed in this process as I felt more able to understand the complexities of mental health. Symptoms I'd only ever read about and memorised from textbooks became embodied. *Ah, so that is what it feels like.* I knew I would never have to memorise them again.

Many clients suffering trauma come to me with radical amalgamations of body sensations, disturbing images and supernatural perceptions. They are convinced they have a dire disease, tumour, chemical imbalance or electrical disturbance of the brain, serious blood derangement or psychotic illness. They know something is wrong or unreal, as if they're living inside another body, or they have multiple characters living within. At times, they hear voices, ringing or buzzing in their ears, their name being called; or they see objects move, distorted face in mirrors, feel the sensation of ants crawling on their sweaty or dry skin, walls closing in; and typically accompanied by inexplicable terror. I identified with only a fraction of these perturbing trauma precipitants. The list, I discovered, was infinite.

As time passed, the intensity subsided, and I had more and more symptom-free days. Even now, they resurface intermittently and spread rapidly like an infection through my body. I feel a hot flooding of discomfort, and immediately, I'm not present. I shut down and retreat from the world. My eyes can see out, but I'm locked inside. Other times, it feels like a knife is stabbing at my chest, acute and harrowing, forcing me to double-over, clutch at my heart, as I massage the shield of breast and ribs trying to ease the ache into a bearable tenderness that slowly dissipates. Without the expertise of my profession, I would have been flummoxed by the sequelae of my trauma.

Trauma and psychiatry are enmeshed. The severity of trauma exists on a spectrum, as is the timespan of our lives over which traumatic incidents occur. These can range from moments of minor transgression to major abuse and neglect, which most of us recognise having experienced, but often don't discuss because we're precluded by shame, guilt and the desire to forget.

Trauma triggers the brain's alarm system nestled in the amygdala as well as our stress response. This induces a cascade of hormones, chemicals, neurotransmitters and second messenger systems, which protect us and motivate our fight, flight or freeze responses. When this is repeated or prolonged, it causes toxic damage to neurons, disrupting our brain's anatomy and neurocircuitry.

Fear, uncertainty or insecurity caused by something as simple as a mother screaming at her toddler, a threatening teacher, angry boss or bullying friend can set off the inbuilt alarm and at times, leave it malfunctioned and easily set-off. This explains our feelings of danger and angst at anything, everything or nothing at all. We find it near impossible to function normally, preferring the safety of solitude or the familiar. When we are re-exposed to further trauma, a disturbing vicious cycle is created that confirms we have no control, that we are shameful, sordid and unlovable.

Trauma can permanently redefine our views, feelings and interactions. Early-life trauma and the ensuing neurotoxic effects of anxiety have a profoundly negative impact on structural and functional brain development. These changes are visible on neuroimages of brains in traumatised individuals. A few of the findings include over-activity within the amygdala (which acts as the brain's alarm), a smaller hippocampus (which is the brain area responsible for learning and memory) and less right-left brain integration (which helps us verbalise our emotions). Because other factors such as genetics, the trauma itself, unique temperaments and the environment are implicated, different people are affected in diverse ways. Approaches to treatment and individual responses are also not the same for everyone.

With the trauma spectrum in mind, loss begins the moment we are born when the umbilical cord is cut, and we are deprived of the warmth, predictability and perfection of the womb and a sense of oneness with our mothers.

In the normal developmental process of separation and individuation, our every crawl, waddle and step further away from our parental figures (if there are any), is a micro-loss, setting us on our grief journey. Time only grows this realisation of non-existent ideal love, recycling our hurt feelings through the wheels of disappointing relationships and dejecting life happenings.

Our confidence becomes dented, we feel incapable, we risk less to avoid additional setbacks; and finally, some of us may be unable to battle the unfair moments in our lives. Potential future upheaval can feel too hard.

But learning to tolerate what is depressing and difficult makes us stronger, more accepting and resilient. We grow our mental flexibility and self-compassion. We become less expectant and entitled. When we debunk the unlovable myth that underpins rejection sensitivity, our self-worth and self-esteem can begin to grow. We begin to find gratitude in the minutiae of goodness the world offers us, knowing that it is a gift, not a given; a fortune, not a forever. We learn to stop minimizing hurt and feeling guilty for it; neither do we pretend, ignore or try to escape any longer. Instead, we are called to expand ourselves, freeing all emotions so we can observe our interpersonal processes with greater self-awareness.

If we're lucky to have had nurturing beginnings that jump-started our ability to manage, self-soothe and cope with our emotions, we may be less inclined to resort to unhealthy defences. This might mean we have fewer tumultuous relationships, anger issues and moments of zoning out. We are also less likely to suffer from disturbed memories, distrust, addictions, instability and poor self-worth.

It's normal to yearn for a utopian life, but ultimately, we have to save our own lives by palliating our grief at perfection's non-existence. We are called upon to develop a healthy pessimism.

When we begin to understand and appraise situations realistically, we are better equipped to choose the most appropriate and effective action. Simply put, if something is good for us, we move towards it; and if it's bad, we move away. This black-and-white approach can assist us to make decisions. But life is not without its grey areas, so this can be limiting. So how do we know if something is good for us? Sometimes, situations are ambiguous and complex, with both pros and cons. As we mature though, we begin to accept that love and hate can co-exist. We start to learn how to be with paradoxical emotions.

Of course, this can be confusing, particularly when our boundaries and trust have been violated due to past trauma. If we've suffered severe abuse, our survival instinct kicks in to stop us feeling like we will be extinguished in moments of fuzzy uncertainty. When we have been abused by a loved one, we manage the inexplicable hurt and confusion in unconscious ways by idealising and protecting them and sometimes, even taking blame for their actions. In this way, we avoid feeling the devastating truth of being unloved. At other times, we may devalue abusers to justify our hatred, but are left feeling like the nasty ones.

Trauma impacts how we live in the aftermath. My own traumatic circumstances have given me a far greater understanding of how it trails us. I can relate wholeheartedly and empathise with those enduring similar experiences.

But in my work, I am frequently challenged to deal with clients who have endured extreme trauma, including physical and sexual abuse. I cannot profess to know firsthand how it feels, but as a therapist who has counselled survivors, I have some idea of how it affects peoples' lives. I have no trouble recognising the symptoms or making the diagnosis or deciding on a treatment of choice – no, not at all. I have read the textbooks and the latest journals. I have attended the lectures and the conferences. I have all the knowledge. But this information is only a fraction of what makes us who we are; the rest comes from experience – living life – not what's written in the books. 'Life is the lesson,' as Dad would say. I can attest to it.

For such clients, I often feel like a total fraud trying to express my understanding and empathy at what they might be going through. No matter what I say, or how I try to say it, I feel foolish and as if my statements only minimise the impact of their experiences. It is impossible to show understanding and give the appropriate acknowledgement to someone who has experienced a trauma of such magnitude.

I would hate a client to feel I haven't offered enough sincere empathy, recognition and validation of their suffering. At times, I say nothing because I don't have the right words, or any words for that matter. In those moments, I hope they are still able to feel respected, heard and held, as I hold the space for their pain.

Losing my dad under such shocking circumstances gave me a small window of insight into the impact of trauma. Still, it was not the kind of trauma that violates the individual's sense of self and rips apart their expected and fundamental need for trust. Basic trust lies at the heart of every meaningful relationship. Without it, there is no relationship. And without the trusting relationship, there is no foundation on which to build a stable and integrated sense of self.

When trust goes, everything goes; and sometimes, getting it back can feel impossible.

But it isn't.

CHAPTER 31

Re-Learning Trust

When trust is disturbed or destroyed, we're compelled to restart. We have to learn to trust again, this time, on a fractured base.

What is it that has to be rebuilt when we lose faith in people?

Most of us who have moved beyond the emotional age of a toddler can endure the upset of getting served the wrong flavour of ice cream or not being invited to a party. These aren't generally atrocities that leave us shuddering at people, detesting ourselves, withdrawing, isolating or on the extreme side, contemplating suicide.

Trust allows us to feel soothed and is a safe haven in which we can be vulnerable. It forms the foundation on which we can stand steady and spread our wings as we leap into the abyss. Trust breeds trust. Each time A follows B, the sun comes up in the morning, stars appear in a clear night's sky and fish inhabit our oceans, we become secure enough to open the doors we have kept shut, explore unknowns, adventure hungrily, surprise our taste buds, love freely and satiate our talents. We can let go of our fears that ill-fortune follows us like a bad smell.

The caress of trust is light and airy, warm and summery. It's a smile on a familiar face and the feeling of comfortably letting go, knowing that our fall will be broken. It is a father running after a child trying out a bike without training wheels for the first time, or a mother holding our hand while we wait at the dentist. It is so simple yet so good for us.

Some consider trust a naïve response to life. It can make us easy to fool and be disarmed. If it is used malevolently, it can deceive and mislead people into life's dark, haunting corners.

As life and relationships adhere to certain rules, our trust is crafted in pattern repetition so we can lock in the predictability of sameness. But it is readily shattered, often never reinstated, when we are hurt by those who are meant to love us, often when someone with power uses it for self-serving interests.

Those who've suffered such betrayal become hardened. They shield their emotions to create a protective barrier to dull the sensitivity to pain, just like soles of the feet become thickened after walking miles across rugged terrain. Distrust resets their barometer of realistic expectations as a protective device. This response is, of course, understandable; but it is a damaged response to the world.

Trauma causes injury, damaging our brain's biology and psychology. It severs neuronal connections, which in turn tarnishes beliefs and splinters relationships. Despite expanding our knowledge of the many biological factors that underpin the presenting symptoms of trauma, we're no further along the path of improving human kindness, and hence, we continue to inflict and experience pain.

Medication used correctly has its place in helping to treat the organic ramifications of trauma. But effective therapy performs two important jobs – it integrates neuronal disconnect and delivers human benevolence. The relationship between therapist and client becomes a safe base from which a traumatised person can begin to explore again. It provides a corrective experience as it heals – not in its promise of perfection – but in its consistency, care and tolerance. Therapists hold a position of privilege and responsibility, which needs to be guarded and respected. The range of emotions unleashed by trauma can be recognised and released in therapy. Here we are, safe enough to express previously disallowed negative feelings which caused us to unconsciously create and enact different personas. We might experience the roles we have inhabited as hearing 'other' voices in our head which instruct us to do bad things or tell us we're awful. This is a defence known as splitting-off, or separating ourselves from negative feeling states that can feel contradictory to ourselves. It helps us shift the responsibility of badness so we can more easily like and tolerate ourselves.

There is no simple answer to what works best when it comes to therapy as effective treatment depends on so many factors. It is important that those of us treating trauma understand this complexity and be less prescriptive. Each person's situation should be assessed as a unique case.

Some might argue that the structured, manualised and predominantly skills-based therapies (e.g., Cognitive Behaviour Therapy or Dialectical Behaviour Therapy) don't necessarily explore the deeper factors which account for the underlying cause of the presenting symptoms. There is value in learning strategies to tolerate distress, but I've heard clients express frustration at not understanding the origins and meaning of these feelings. The surgical removal of a cancer is generally followed by chemotherapy or radiation to prevent recurrence. However, when a patient has a brief course of therapy to target a set of distressing symptoms, this isn't always followed up with a course of extensive and exploratory therapy to empower the patient and prevent the same health problem from arising in the future.

At the same time, exploratory, dynamic therapies can be triggering and unsettling; and I wouldn't recommend them for everyone. If a person has any doubts, I'd suggest they discuss the options in detail with a trained mental health professional. Therapists might focus on building rapport, developing and enhancing soothing strategies with clients prior to engaging in further probing work.

When I treat clients, I aim for honesty because it is important to me that they feel my sincerity in wanting to help them. I'm always mindful of how my feelings, thoughts and experiences might impact on the person sitting in front of me. I try to offer clients ample room to explore and generate personal conclusions. If they need or request it, I'll offer an opinion or direction. Other purist psychotherapists prefer to remain a voiceless blank slate to promote a client's expression of their unconscious thoughts and fantasies, so they keep all personal information hidden. Used with free association, a client is encouraged to say whatever comes to mind.

My approach is to allow clients to get to know me while upholding professional boundaries, of course, especially if I feel they have pre-conceived ideas about me that are noticeably impacting our rapport.

I find my clients are comforted when I share similar experiences from my own life and divulge my imperfections. I only do this if it feels fitting, and I think it could be helpful. The appropriate use of self-disclosure can bring a sense of ease into the room. If I choose to disclose parts of my life to my clients, I am always thoughtful and measured in this process, and I never do so frivolously or gratuitously. But I respect beliefs and therapeutic methods which do not, just as I equally respect human differences. Ultimately, the test is whether the particular therapy and the relationship is supporting a client in reclaiming their sound mental health.

Humans are born and develop within relationships, which means the therapy relationship is a powerful place to facilitate healing and personal growth. I'm not specifically trained in psychotherapy, but self-study and experience have guided my eclectic, relational approach to my clients. A benevolent relationship and solid rapport, in my opinion, are as important as the science.

I always note my own feelings and sensations as well as the subtle and obvious interactions in the room. This is the microcosm, representing my client's exchanges in their macrocosm, or the outside world in which they live. It is confronting to evaluate ourselves. Self-exposure takes time because trust is the foundation on which it depends. People need to feel safe to explore. Otherwise, they might feel criticised or attacked, and that will only make them want to withdraw, defend themselves or escape.

In my own therapy journey, I have worked to release my feelings of being not good enough and unlovable. I also needed to develop more trust in relationships and the ability to sit with my difficult emotions. I have become better at not running away because my tendency is to avoid conflict and other peoples' anger. In my life, I have felt suffocated and disgusting in my skin, a disturbing self-loathing and melancholy. Looking in the mirror, I have felt nausea, wanting to vomit. The agitation has, at times, been overbearing as I fixated on every curve of my body, unhappy with the sight of me. There has never been anything wrong or unbeautiful about me, but my past trauma caused me to lodge my deepest shame in my body. As I ran and avoided, I projected my frustration on everyone else's inability to manage *their* lives.

My greatest epiphany in therapy was the discovery that within my hard shell is a vulnerable core, a Pandora's box that holds my wealth of sadness and deep pain. I overcame the fear of opening it, losing control and not coping. I have since been able to help clients at a similar junction, by cushioning and containing their release of raw emotion. This process leaves us open as we bear a graze that stings outside in the warm incubator of the therapy room. After a therapy session, clients might need time to transition back into their daily lives, similar to the bubble of grief I found myself in after losing my dad, in which living normally was difficult in my vulnerable and disconnected state. Just as I needed time to settle, so I know my clients do too.

I've had clients question the usefulness of therapy, perplexed at the unsettling that can occur. I tell them that it's like reopening a wound that has been there for a long time, but the wound has not been well mended. I explain that with each session, the wound is opened again – causing deep pain, which is the unsettling they feel. But with time, it does heal, leaving only a small scar, unique and interestingly beautiful, a subtle reminder of their pain, struggle and progress.

For many, this is a challenging process. Most of us want to avoid it at all costs. We prefer to remain in pain and for the wound to be left unopened, despite it being visible and more grotesque. Without knowing someone's story, I don't judge this antipathy. Change is a process, as is the readiness to engage. But for those who are brave enough to open the door into the unknown depths of their mind, they get to enjoy the rewards of gaining control of what has felt to be uncontrollable.

I began my therapy in South Africa during my training as a psychiatrist, and it helped me through my early days of mothering and emigration. I wasn't ready to let go of my therapist and needed a weaning period. I persisted with a year of phone consults. The COVID-19 pandemic has normalised online therapy with the help of technology, but at the time, I found it less personal and so sought a local therapist.

Of course, medication and therapy aren't the only ways in which to manage our mental health and wellbeing. It's also not my only way. But what we manage internally aids external change. Unfortunately, the stigma that surrounds mental health furthers psychological illness by creating dis-ease in accepting that help is needed and reaching out for it.

Managing our minds is an ongoing process which runs parallel to and is intertwined with everyday life. Daily, we confront experiences that span from minute fractures in expectations, to gross violations of our basic human needs, wants and rights – such as trust, safety, freedom and love.

Self-development is painful and time consuming, but we receive the benefits of becoming empowered and accepting who we are. When we first learn any new skill, like riding a bike, we have to focus intently at first. But with enough practice, the skill becomes implicit, engrained and automatic. The same is true for emotion regulation and behaviour management skills.

Achieving mental strength, focus and flexibility makes dealing with life's challenges easier. Acceptance doesn't necessarily mean agreement, but rather the ability to untangle and proceed with self-compassion and less judgement.

Despite the ruptures in my past, I've learnt how to manage trust and see light and love around me. I avoid what isn't necessarily all bad but which I know is not serving me. I can live with an open heart despite the actions of others – including those who may have had a hand in taking my dad's life.

I am not minimising or excusing awful, unlawful behaviour. I have experienced the ramifications of trauma, sitting opposite clients whose pain cannot be worded, but felt only with voiceless communication. All I can do in those moments is provide trusted human kind-heartedness and care, without any personal agenda. Yes, as a doctor, clients remunerate me financially for my support, which some 'healers' may find innately juxtaposed to their rescuing drive; but it is an essential, learnt boundary and self-care mechanism to be modelled. It doesn't negate care. I have moved from rescuer to supporter and guide.

When bad things happen to us, we lose trust. But we can start again.

I have had to learn to trust that I'm a good person despite some poor actions in the past. That I can be helped by more than one person and have multiple successful relationships. That I will be hurt, but I can also heal; and healing makes me a better, kinder and more compassionate human being.

I am here to let you know that if I could get there, so can you.

CHAPTER 32

Global Trauma
Triggered by COVID-19

I'd known Kelvin, a man in his fifties, for a few years. His struggle with low self-esteem since childhood had peaked in his teens. In comparison to his brothers, he'd always felt robbed by being encoded with the crappier DNA that cursed him with, in his eyes, 'detestable looks and physicality.' His sense of self-disgust bordered on a dysmorphia. I could relate, having projected my poor self-value into my body, which had likewise caused me to despise it.

I thought it strange that he deliberately sought a child psychiatrist. His theory and hope, he explained, was that a child psychiatrist, being more familiar with a child's mind, would be suitably qualified to rework his inner child. Kelvin had an extreme health anxiety and fear of dying. He was terrified of abandoning his only son, who was twelve. In his early thirties, Kelvin had lost his father tragically when he fell from a height and was hospitalised but never came out. Kelvin bookmarked it as the day he lost all confidence, became consumed with fear of death and perturbed by the slightest change in his body.

Towards the end of 2019, in one of our sessions, he began to obsess about his fear of a new virus.

Frustrated, I offered, 'I think you are over-reacting and allowing this to play into your overwhelming anxiety and fears of death.'

Personally, I couldn't wait for 2019 and its strife to be over. It was my year of doom. The dawn of a new decade – 2020 – was bringing with it promise, and I didn't want the wheels on Kelvin's latest choo-choo train of disaster to squash my excitement. I am a doctor and regard viruses as normal, seasonal or yearly; and if at all a problem, medical science was advanced and would have impressive solutions. I near-laughed at his talk about supply chain issues, years of sickness, deaths, falling economies and a lack of toilet paper!

I thought he had finally lost his mind and was being completely ridiculous. I told him there was no way a virus would shut down the world and explained that extreme anxiety could cause us to lose touch with reality, making our worrying thoughts and beliefs seem to border on the delusional.

You won't be surprised to learn that since that day, I value, if not seek, all of Kelvin's predictions.

I can forgive my naivety – I had never lived through a pandemic before. At the time, it seemed inconceivable that a micro-organism, COVID-19, would implode our world. And yes, I've humbly and profusely apologised to Kelvin for shunning his incredible foresight.

Two thousand nineteen had been one of the toughest years for many Australians as our landscape was devastated by bushfires that killed billions of animals, destroyed approximately fifty million acres of bushland and caused nearly forty fatalities. The afflicted communities and entire country of onlookers were despondent and completely fatigued. No-one could imagine we were at the foothills of further catastrophe.

Had anyone been told what the world would look like today, they would never have believed it. But COVID-19 has bit its teeth into us and certainly cemented the notion that life isn't fair and doesn't ever go to plan.

Our human resilience and adaptability have been stress-tested. On a basic level, we've all had to change or suspend plans and find new ways of doing old things. In my field of work, telehealth consultations have now become the norm rather than the exception. Some may find this more convenient and accessible, whilst others are put off by its lack of personability. I find it harder to concentrate in sessions, and I am more exhausted at the end of a day of consultations. It's tough to diagnose a patient without the enhanced nonverbal cues of being face to face.

COVID has escalated the mental health crisis. I too have felt the depressed mood in the air and lack of motivation that accompanies loss and feelings of hopelessness. The swell of my bleak outlook lessened with each optimistic statistic, a drop in case numbers, or statements of promise like no further lockdowns (or should we have called them lockups?).

COVID has reminded humans of our fragility and the

gift of health. The restrictions on activities that provide our lives with meaning and purpose have caused our general mood to flatline. Not knowing what tomorrow will be has made it challenging to maintain a positive outlook.

A dictionary of new terms has sprouted such as *social distancing* and *super-spreader.* Now they're colloquial, but pre-COVID might have brought to mind notions of living far apart from friends or a great margarine.

COVID has exposed our human vulnerabilities, the tricks our minds can play and our limitations as we've had to try and understand the complexities of microbiology and infectious disease transmission, all while our bodies fight to stay healthy. The list of system gaps and failures is as long as the breadth of the divide it's created between people – each an expert with an opinion on what to believe, who to blame and how best to manage the situation.

Never, in even my craziest fantasies, could I have imagined the advent of this chemical warfare. Many times, I've considered the pandemic to be our generation's World War III. While driving along quiet roads to work, as most people were isolating, I've tried to imagine living through the Great Depression and World Wars, visualizing similarities – the depressed mood, rationing of supplies, seeing relatives go to war and not return, desperately wishing for an end, but feeling as if it would never happen. It's depressing to see desolate pavements lined with empty shops and a few sombre souls hidden behind a face mask – an item which, until recently, we only saw in pollution-conscious Asian countries.

Urging (or enforcing) vaccination has been contentious as we were called to the battle lines with unsighted trust in those who had done the research, risk the trials, standing together as a community, a country and a world to facilitate our collective survival. As in battle, there have sadly been casualties; but hard too has been the segregating and often angry anti-vaccination sentiments, and what has felt like a very singular stance. I've thought about the soldiers' boarding planes or trains, not knowing whether they would return, but prioritising the welfare of others ahead of themselves.

How I've missed the world as it was before COVID. Yes, the lockdowns slowed us down for a while and made us think about the value of family time. They were a great reminder to be mindful, but the lessons were short-lived and diminished by the financial ruins, job losses and deaths. Many tech industries derived extreme wealth by providing options to communicate from a distance but have also preyed on the anxiety generated by our close contact with other humans, propagating the idea of living safely within a virtual world.

I long for the days of carefree travel and the closeness of people, unfussed by a cough or sneeze. I'm nostalgic for certainty – at least simple givens like going to work every day or my children being dropped off at the school gate. I get sentimental remembering my holiday to Vietnam immediately before COVID, as I recall the bustle of people and busy roads. I was fearless eating food prepared by street vendors who didn't have running water to wash utensils, let alone sanitisers to disinfect the low plastic tables we sat around. How wonderful it was to sit without a care in a theatre or cinema and walk through a museum without a facemask. I loved attending my daughters' dance concerts in packed halls and the netball games on cheering, parent-encircled courts.

As a child adolescent psychiatrist, I initially saw COVID as an opportunity for our youth to face *real* adversity. Staying home for lengthy periods forced them to stretch their imaginations and tolerate frustration as they found ways to entertain themselves, feeding their need for constant external stimulation.

This has been the chance to regain perspective, especially if we have never experienced any real trials in life. Unfortunately, what I've witnessed is how excess screen time became the space filler for bored children and teenagers in place of in-classroom learning and socialising. Technology and social media provided fertile soil for the increase in online bullying and exclusion. A young client explained how her friends would spitefully and deliberately lock her out of chat rooms and group chats, causing her to feel desperate and panicked. Of course, there are always two (or more) sides to a story; but no matter the reason, it's agonising to witness another's hurt, especially when they're too young to accurately identify the likely passive-aggressive nature of these acts.

I have barely been able to juggle the demands of work and supervise my daughters' home schooling at the same time, so they have fallen behind, as many others have too.

In Australia, where the government has provided financial aid in the form of Jobkeeper and Jobseeker, older teens and young adults often preferred the comfort of the couch, earning more money by sitting watching Netflix than by working. Who can blame them for finding lucky loopholes in the system to their benefit in such a dark and depressing time?

Mental health presentations have increased during the pandemic for various reasons. For many who suffered with pre-existing problems, it has unquestionably compounded them – for example, increasing germ obsessions and cleaning compulsions in the context of a spreading virus. But in others, COVID provided a legitimate reason for the socially anxious to isolate, whilst attributing their fears to the risk of becoming infected. I can empathise, knowing the shame of a mental health stigma; and having an acceptable reason that feels less personal or weak reduces our feelings of humiliation. Anxious children have found safety in home-schooling. Many have refused to return to school when it was safe to do so. The socialites became depressed. The reclusive, avoidant and the multitasker enjoyed working from home; less so those who need human connection or the structure and routine of the office. The ramifications and difficulties are certain to continue through this pandemic and beyond.

But I draw on the lessons I learned when I lost my father. The rains of suffering and loss have to drown us in sadness before gratitude can sprout. I'm immensely thankful to have a job, my health (even after a COVID infection) and most of my family. I am relieved I was able to be physically present to bury Dad, as I know how many others have been denied this closure. In other ways, I'm pleased Dad has been spared the financial suffering COVID would have wrought on his already tired business. I've often said to Mum that if anything could have forced Dad to take his life, this debacle would have been it.

I'm appreciative of medical science and the scientists

who've pioneered vaccines, the decision-makers who faced the hindsight-critics claiming they could have done a better job.

Everyone has felt the lack of control COVID has brought to our lives, and this has ignited anxiety. We are all doing our best to take it back. Denial and paranoid delusions have given life to conspiracy theories, the obsessive control freaks have gone on hoarding sprees, and the light-hearted among us have hidden behind memes and jokes. Our defences have varied, but our reasoning has been the same – we're all just trying to make sense of the inexplicable.

Each one of us has suffered in unity. The human race's power and potential at times appears minute in comparison to this tiny virus. This has created the opportunity for us to reflect and resume humility. There are many messages in the madness, but for me, the greatest has been what I've learned from a joint experience of suffering. It has tied us together and pushed us apart; made us either compassionate or critical; at times grateful, then grouchy and cantankerous; feel deprived when help has been offered to others but not to us.

The unprecedented nature of events, which left us no time to prepare, has been traumatic and terrifying, just like my trauma of losing my dad. I have seen the pattern repeat itself – the reflex of denial, followed by the emotional flurry, anger and bargaining, the tiring ruminating thought processes, the endless seeking of answers to guide the way forward, the epic losses and insurmountable sadness. Like in war, as in death, we grieve forever.

Suffering brings about change but asks us to be

pliable. It is the gateway to both personal and communal growth. Life and hardship are synonymous, like pain and joy. As with thinking, we are stifled if it is too black and white. Our mission is to learn to hold the extremes in one hand.

The trauma of this suffering has instilled anxiety, even a form of PTSD. The constant taking a step forward, only to take three back, destroy our confidence and trust. No matter the event, the underlying psychology of trauma is the same. To ride this storm, we need the tools of awareness and resilience.

I like to believe that the world is circular, that suffering comes and goes, along with fashion trends, like the merry-go-round we enjoyed as children. Change is uncomfortable, but it's a certainty – like death – that we cannot flee. Suffering leaves wounds, but these heal and form scars which build character. We can't hide them, but we become remarkable in our imperfection because of them.

Coronavirus has turned off the light in our lives as we knew them, but all we need is a small flame of faith to reignite the fires that can shine light again on the world.

I have seen the end of the world.

I saw it the day I walked into the room where my father was murdered. And so trust me when I say that the world will be illuminated again. It will be a new world – not better or worse – but different.

I cannot dare predict the outcome of this global trauma. Time will write the completed narrative.

But at school, my Jehovah's Witness friends would sometimes read me the biblical books of Revelations and explain how the scriptures clearly prophesised the nearing of doomsday and end of the world. It would scare me, and I'd run to Dad, needing his reassurance!

'Is this true?' I'd ask, panicked. Dad always replied in the same way.

'Lisa, I am not a hundred per cent sure, but I do know that similar fears have been expressed from when I was a child, and I am sure for years before that…and yet, see the world continues.'

His answer always comforted me.

CHAPTER 33

Small Steps Cover Great Distances

Molly's husband came alone to see me for the initial appointment because Molly was in hospital for the second time in quick succession. We were not to know that there would be numerous hospital admissions over the years to come.

She'd been diagnosed with bipolar mood disorder. 'Oh, and trauma,' he'd added.

When I began treating her, she did not disclose much about her past trauma. If only I'd had more information, I would have prioritised treating it.

Over the years, Molly and her husband managed the cycling manic, depressed and psychotic symptoms with adequate medication and therapy. But the impact of her childhood trauma had created a deep well of shame, worthlessness, guilt and sadness in her which overflowed with disappointment whenever her family of origin denied the trauma had ever happened. It can be just as, or even more, painful for a trauma victim to be disbelieved and unprotected by the non-abusers than it is to experience the abuse.

Prior to her diagnosis Molly was a capable and successful woman. She struggled to accept her mental illness was a long-term prognosis. I had to frequently remind her that she remained that intelligent person, but she battled to bring the two images of herself – pre and post diagnosis – together in her mind. The months of hospital admissions fused into years of sickness, and with it came many losses – of her home, career, friends and family. Molly expressed her anguish at being ostracised once she was labelled as mentally ill. But sometimes she saw the humour in the way people treated her.

'It's as if they think I'm contagious, and I'll give them bipolar,' she would say.

Her mental state fluctuated, but when she was settled (still without job and home) she embarked on new challenges. One of these was Tai Chi. Unfortunately, Molly's best intentions didn't last, and she became unwell again soon after starting this new activity.

At one of our appointments, she relayed a moment in the class filled with many high-flying, well-to-do women.

'I was like them once upon a time,' she remarked sadly, not entirely comfortable letting go of her ideal self-image.

She was animated and articulate as she described how she'd stood at the back of the class, shifting her weight anxiously from one leg to the other, completely dishevelled from days of not showering, her hair unkempt, her nails dirty at the end of yellow cigarette-stained fingers. She'd been chewing gum obsessively in tune with her torturous and ruminating thoughts, completely oblivious of anyone else, unable to follow the Tai Chi moves. She laughed at herself as she relayed this to me, using humour as a mature defence.

'Then two of these women approached the teacher – a lovely person who's had her own difficulties which she's spoken openly about in class,' Molly relayed, mimicking the two women's facial expressions. They'd made no effort to hide their disgust as they asked the instructor if there was 'something wrong' with Molly.

'Yes, there is,' the instructor replied, unimpressed by their lack of compassion. 'And she is doing the best she can.' She then dismissed them to check how Molly was doing.

Small acts of kindness like these can make all the difference to someone who is battling with mental health challenges.

In our sessions, Molly would relentlessly orbit her many mistakes and how her life had gone fully south. She had lost her home and her career, when her husband decided that moving to a quieter place was better for her mental health since many friends, colleagues and family members struggled to understand her mental illness.

'Sometimes, others' fears make them step away. Mental illness can be confronting, and it can be difficult to know the right thing to say or do. Perhaps it explains them stepping back?' I consoled. I always did my best to soothe her hurt by helping her explore other potential reasons for those close to her having distanced themselves.

On one particular day, however, I noticed a slight change in the way she spoke about herself. It became clear that she was taking small steps which added up to a steady improvement, indicating that she was slowly coming to terms with her illness. She seemed to have more self-compassion as she forgave herself and made a distinction between her being and her illness. She was not bipolar, but *had* bipolar.

This was just the beginning. Molly's nascent shift in attitude began to pave the way for her to rebuild a life again. It was not the magical movie ending where she miraculously got back her massive house and thriving career. But she proudly told me that she'd attended church on Christmas Day and had sent out Christmas cards for the first time in years. She joked about how the minister had asked whether she was 'cured' when her husband mentioned she'd had a lengthy battle with mental health issues and remarked on how people expected her to get on with life because she looked okay.

'People seem to understand frailty when they can see a physical disability. Mental health is different.'

She'd lost her picture-perfect life, like an expensive artwork for all to admire. That life with all its trappings had failed to depict the story of the troubled artist – until it all collapsed.

I have deep compassion for patients like Molly because I wasn't much different from her for many years, always hiding my shame behind a veil of achievement and apparent perfection. In my own life, nothing has felt more liberating than when I broke the shackles of upholding pretence and began to live closer to my truth. My goal is always to appreciate and validate clients, friends and family for just being themselves.

But it has taken me time to come to this place of

understanding and appreciation of those who are mentally unwell. As a young registrar starting my psychiatry training, I found sick patients who needed hospital admission intriguing. It's not every day that you get to observe another person having a detailed two-way-conversation with themselves, or hear stories of how they were poisoned by relatives who had cameras in their bedroom observing their every move, or that they are the Messiah who came to save the world.

One of my patients at the Helen Joseph Hospital with a schizoaffective disorder (mood and psychosis combined) loved to watch every episode of *The Bold and Beautiful* at 11am. Every day, he'd take his seat on one of the few worn couches and chairs that were scantily dispersed in the patients' shared television room. Fewer pieces of furniture were strategically placed because it was impossible to predict when someone might get violent and fling a chair or table across the room or worse, at a staff member or fellow patient. The only, almost antique, tiny TV was hoisted high on the wall within a shatter-proof Perspex box. It was often impossible to see or hear the TV, especially if someone was screaming. Yet patients would spend hours staring blankly at the screen, mostly content in their own worlds, and often quietly harmonious and thoughtful of each other – you could discern in their few words and gestures. At mealtimes, some patients would stand back to make space for those needier and more unwell, often intuitively knowing who was less tolerant. Others would share their food with a hungrier patient who'd gobbled theirs too quickly. I witnessed many of these small acts of kindness amongst inpatients.

In *The Bold and the Beautiful*, the character Ridge Forrester was dating an intelligent, attractive, long-haired brunette psychiatrist called Dr Taylor. Whenever I'd see my patient, he'd call out loudly, 'Dr Maylor, Dr Maylor! You are on the TV and dating Ridge Forrester! You are famous!'

Any health professional who has studied medicine and psychiatry could fill a book with the many stories of our colourful patients. We all share this amazing and privileged career of caring for people with mental health issues.

Being a doctor has taught me how to deal with unplanned moments of crisis despite all our human efforts and best intentions to maintain a structured diary and a perfect work-life balance. Unforeseen everyday life events happen and throw us around again like a chair flung across a room that no-one sees coming. We all have to regroup, readjust and realign.

Despite my extensive training in expecting the unpredictable, I wasn't prepared for losing my father in the way that I did. My years of coping with uncertainty – which has always been the only certainty – by multitasking, compartmentalising and making time in therapy to process my emotions helped me more than I realised and provided some of the recourses I needed to manage.

The longer I trained and worked in psychiatry, the less illness fascinated me. I began to understand and see patients as people. The psychotic patient became just another 'ordinary' person with a story – often an awful one. I was often simply grateful it wasn't mine.

One day, whilst driving with my two girls, I stopped at

a traffic light and was excited to see a man I knew from past admissions at a mental health unit for his chronic schizophrenia. As he passed my car, he turned and spat on my windshield. My children were flabbergasted especially when I reacted by simply squirting water to wipe the saliva from the glass. I explained he was not well and did not know better. His action wasn't malicious, and it didn't really inconvenience me. I had the more privileged life. Truthfully, I was glad to see he was well enough not to be hospitalised.

I've often wondered how I would have managed similar adverse life circumstances to some of my patients. Perhaps I too would have become psychotic or chronically depressed. Though I am conscious of never comparing afflictions and appreciate the complexity of mental illness, in those moments, I've quietly thanked my parents, who were as far from perfect as the earth from the sun, for somehow giving me enough of a safe base (and reasonable genetics) to survive the hardships I have faced.

As an adult, I was diagnosed with ADHD (Attention Deficit and Hyperactivity Disorder). Medication has helped me. Looking back over the years, I see that my dogged determination has often trumped the impact of my symptoms, but I have frequently been despondent and wondered how others recalled information after only reading it once when I had to go over it multiple times. The frustration of throwing everything out of my bag daily to find a key or a credit card hasn't lessened. But now that I know it's my attention deficit, it makes more sense, so I can have more compassion and become less aggravated with myself.

Completing this book rates amongst my greatest achievements. I made a promise to myself that it wouldn't be yet another project started, but not completed.

A young client with ADHD told me that she'd been discouraged from studying law by another health professional who cited ADHD as a preclusion. In that moment, it felt fitting and helpful to share my story with her.

It has become my passion to give others the experience of a leg up and to be a support person who believes in their ability. All too often, we are incapable of seeing our own potential and feel defective. Providing clients with truthful and balanced feedback about the positive perceptions I have of them can be uplifting and motivating. It's all there, inside, the qualities needed to succeed. They just need unlocking, and sometimes, my clients simply need the confidence to take a chance – as do we all.

Fear of failure and the judgement of others inhibit the most competent among us from trying and reaching our potential. It's my experience that *others* generally don't care or aren't looking. And if they are, they often leverage the downfall of another to make themselves feel better. I don't preach that anyone can achieve everything or anything, or that we should ever regard ourselves as perfect. I don't encourage people to have unrealistic expectations of grandeur or be cheery and as gleeful as an evangelic minister or self-help guru.

I teach and advocate for each of us to be objective, not simply judgemental, when making a self-evaluation.

We also need to nurture tolerance of the process, which is a life-long journey that never follows a straight line. Asking questions is the only path to finding answers, but we need vulnerability and courage to explore. We find our pot of gold of acceptance and strength when we work with our vulnerability, overcome our shame and no longer feel the need to hide, try or compare.

Differences aside, as humans, we are fundamentally the same; and all face our battles and obstacles – inside our bodies, minds and in the world. These qualities don't define who we are, they are what we have to manage – not necessarily fix. Once we accept ourselves as a whole being, we can regard our adversities as the many bags we're given to carry along the way, which turns asking for the help we need into a strength.

Even as we listen to the opinions of others we value, we should test them against our own beliefs, and soak up lessons and advice along the way because it makes us better, not *less than*. We can focus inwards rather than seeking feedback from every direction. We learn the skills of challenging the validity of others' opinions. We can acknowledge our efforts – independent of their magnitude – to be better, not because we aren't already enough, but because they add to what is already there.

Waiting to see results in mental health can be frustrating. Unlike other areas of medicine, progress is often less visible and profound, and so perhaps under-recognised and appears less gratifying. Yet, it is nothing short of magical to witness a dose of lithium settle a manic episode or help a patient overcome a tightly held phobia following a course of exposure and desensitisation therapy.

Treating mental health mirrors life's journey – it is a slow and steady climb, and the successes are often most noticeable in retrospect. The wins can seem small, but when carefully examined under the magnification of context, they are momentous: a socially anxious child going back to school after years of home schooling, another finishing school after numerous admissions to hospital for mental health, someone with longstanding untreated ADHD managing to keep a job for more than a month for the very first time in their lives once medicated, an autistic person completing a college course after being at home for years due to no confidence and social issues, someone managing to be less aggressive, a successful play date, a lasting relationship, fewer panic attacks – the list of examples is endless. In my case, seeing a box cutter as an everyday object again without having it cause me distress and disassociation would be a huge leap forward.

For most people, these might seem like irrelevant events. But having walked alongside so many who have and continue to struggle with their mental health, for me, these are times of pure joy and celebration. I always remind my clients to note these moments as the wins they are because we're generally better at bashing ourselves than we are at congratulating our achievements. Something small is never *nothing*. *Everything* done to accept and master our challenges needs to be applauded. I get goosebumps every time I have the privilege of witnessing my clients' strength in the face of their challenging narratives.

These days I have removed the bar on what I deem as progress and improvement. Anything is something, and I will always see it as a run on the board and cheer my clients on.

I have recognised the anguish in medical students and young psychiatry trainees, who become despondent that their efforts aren't as noticeable and rewarded as their colleagues who excise cancerous tumours or insert pacemakers to thwart arrythmias. They become deflated and useless, and begin to feel like imposters. Their efforts can seem futile, especially when patients are termed frequent flyers due to their recurrent hospitalisations. I understand when they feel like they want to quit. My words of encouragement to them are to trust that time and experience will deliver an ability to recognise what is meaningful and helpful.

These days, I giggle compassionately at the interesting situations that can arise whilst working in mental health. I laugh with my clients and at myself. Each is a person with a unique background story that has brought them to their current bookmark where they are willing to try and write the rest of their book. They are the real-life superheroes.

I think of my dad, who felt his life to be a failure and whose ending was dire. I have to work hard every day to stop my mind from re-entering that dark and demonic cave. I have to imagine my own last chapter for him. One that shines a little brighter.

I have.

It is this.

CHAPTER 34

Rituals and Milestones

'I find it helpful to connect with the negative or stuck energy in my body and then visualise releasing it,' Shaina said from her seat in my consulting rooms. This young woman gave the impression of immense self-confidence but, in truth, was exceptionally vulnerable. She continued, 'Sometimes, writing down my feelings, a memory or a thought on paper and tearing it up or burning it helps me let it go.'

Her family considered her spiritual (meaning weird), but they had no idea of her past sexual traumas. Her ghastly experiences had a terrible impact on her, and she frequently experienced dreadful discomfort and distress as her body recalled what she'd endured.

Shaina's self-constructed rituals are survival tactics she created to cleanse her and remove her feelings of being soiled and disgusting. She had been horribly violated as a child. As a result, throughout her teens and young adulthood, she had engaged in risky behaviour which self-inflicted further trauma. Years of therapy helped her to realise the subconscious motivation of her actions. Yet she continued with grappling to gain control over the feelings of no control as she'd felt during her assaults. But her rituals formalised her progress and were valuable moments of emotional release and compassion on the road to recovery.

She has been able to formally forgive the actions of her younger self by acknowledging the limitations of youth, the impact of her trauma and that she lacked adequate support at crucial times in her life.

In the course of my work, other clients have shared their personal rituals with me which have helped them let go or achieve closure. Rituals seem to alleviate hurt by concretising the impalpable and demarcating the indefinable.

Until I lost my father, I'd never understood the necessity of everyday rituals to help us celebrate, symbolise and validate our experiences. I'd never thought of a birthday cake, an engagement ring or a graduation ceremony as containers of meaning-making. Yet the importance of rituals intensified for me, following my father's death. My farewell of Dad at his grave was a powerful ceremony for me. It allowed me to say goodbye in a tangible way and offered me a passage to the next phase of my journey.

Timing our grieving is essential to any trauma process as is benchmarking our progress. Initially, when we're in survival mode, we might find it impossible to deal with the underlying issues because our mission is to get through every day without falling apart. Although we may feel in control, we're essentially holding on to any form of stability until we can let go and cope.

You could say that my investigation of Dad's death was a grieving ritual and gave me some necessary control over my grief. I needed to understand what seemed illogical in order to place it neatly in a box until I knew what to do with it. I couldn't progress without knowing what I was grieving. Eventually, I realised that Dad's death was never going to make sense. But that insight could only come later. Only then could I mourn the senselessness which became an additional loss in the wake of the first wave of grief.

I was naïve to believe that accepting Dad's death (irrespective of the cause) would free the shackles of my mind. Acceptance was not a single destination that glistened on the other side of the grief-river. It was made up of many lily pads that I would have to move along, sometimes forwards and then backwards. Realising that grieving my father would be a forever process was an important milestone for me. It was another step in the process of achieving a place of processed emotion and objective reflection.

It took me a long time to connect to my sadness. My first moment of release was at Dad's grave, but since then, I've formally honoured him every year on the Hebrew date of his passing known as *Yahrzeit*. The Jewish mourning ritual and custom of lighting a candle, giving charity and reciting prayers have provided me the space to reflect and be mindful, as I consider life, release pain and connect to my father. Having an assigned day also gives me permission to grieve. I'm comforted by his mystical presence. The hurt still stabs me like a knife, but it allows me to feel alive, real and forever attached to my father.

But there are also many days which for no reason I can discern, I grieve, remembering Dad in some way. These moments of reliving his loss or simply recalling my life with him aren't planned or prescribed, and although painful, I always welcome them. They have become my time with Dad.

Death robbed me of Dad's physical presence, but not his memory or the feelings he generates. His loss stopped the clock on creating any further experiences to grow our relationship. Like a giant oak tree that's died and has left a gaping absence in the garden, the emptiness reminds me of the happy moments and his ever-present support that no longer exist in the physical world, but always in my heart.

* * *

On the night of Dad's third *Yahrzeit,* Mum, Cindy, Daniella Rachel and I shared a meal together before lighting the memorial candle. Staring into the flame, we were all quiet, yet Dad's aura and our memories felt tangible. Daniella wept. She asked me to send her a screenshot of her last communication with my father – comments on a Facebook post I'd put up showing our *Shabbat* table, with the caption, '*Last Shabbat of the Year'* (ironically, the last Shabbat with Dad alive). Dad remarked that it looked beautiful, and Daniella had replied. Dad had responded to her comment but not to her final, '*I Love You, Pa.'* It finally made sense that over the past few years, Daniella had insisted that we always replied to her 'I love you's' with the same words.

Losing Dad brought us closer as a family. We hold each other a little more tightly and value our time together. We often share stories and relive memories about Dad. My sister sorted through Dad's belongings after his death, which was like going through his life in paper form. What was once a sad and distressing moment is now a humorous recollection of Dad's obsessive hoarding. These are cathartic, bonding moments that bring him to life when he becomes distant in the course of our daily lives. We also find our solace separately and differently. My sister finds comfort in a pillow she made from one of Dad's old shirts, yet I'm unnerved by it. We each have to find a way to respect everyone's individual needs.

Collectively, our remembrance has evolved from constant tears of grief to, more frequently, celebrations of our achievements and the way we live honouring his many teachings that run like blood in our veins.

My children often speak about the lessons they learned from him and how his absence has illuminated the awareness of his impact. One such insight came from Daniella who said, 'Pa taught me that being rich isn't only about having money, and you don't need a lot to be happy. Real wealth is inside us, not outside. Life is never perfect.'

And that's how I know that his light will never go out.

CHAPTER 35
Finding Closure

It was December 2018, and Dad's visit had come to an end. This time, he'd come alone to Sydney, leaving Mum in South Africa to run his business. He was due to leave the very next day. Somehow, we got into a heated argument, which seemed to be a pattern whenever either he or Mum were about to leave following a stay with us. This often happens when we separate from people we love, as we intuitively protect ourselves, pretending that we can't wait for them to leave.

I was frustrated that Dad had not bought the exact kind of sliced bread I'd asked him to get.

'How hard is it to get the right kind of bread?' I muttered.

He had modelled shaming whilst I was growing up, and now I was doing it to him. Dad was upset he'd disappointed me – he always only ever wanted to help.

I kept attacking him verbally until he retaliated in anger and yelled back, 'Nothing is ever good enough for you!' before he stormed off to his room.

This was a familiar complaint I'd heard frequently over my lifetime. How could he know that my underlying desperate need was for help that would *actually be helpful* in alleviating my heavy load? Unable to tolerate my emotions, I lashed out without kindness or gratitude.

'Don't worry about it! I'll do it myself – I'm used to it!' Another punch to his guts.

Despite the children urging me to say sorry, I stubbornly refused and left Dad alone in his room.

Dad had arrived in Sydney a week before. As a single mother of two primary school-aged girls, I always valued his assistance as well as his company. This time, he had been reluctant to come because he could never justify spending money on *nothing*. He shuddered at being away from the car yard because it meant he was unable to sell vehicles.

'There's no-one else to do it,' he'd say over and over again.

As a result, Dad never planned or took any holidays because he could never afford them. When funds were available, he always had more important bills to pay or essentials to spend them on.

I'd always loved spending time with my father ever since I was a little girl. His company was easy and enjoyable, and our similar humour meant we shared many funny moments, at times laughing hysterically. My two girls felt the same way about him and would look forward to his visits with the same excitement as children eyeing a mountain of presents under the tree on Christmas morning.

Because Dad regarded taking any time off work as

indulgent and was incapacitated by his need to physically be on site, I simply booked him a plane ticket and then notified him of his travel plans. I'd been doing this all my life to ensure that I got time with him. As a child, I'd hidden in the car behind his seat, popping my head out when he was well on his way to work, knowing he'd never turn around and risk being late. It gave me the chance to spend an entire day with him. My mother would often say that only I could get my dad to do things when no-one else could.

Our struggle to not let each other down was mutual.

Despite his reluctance and fear, Dad was always grateful and happy to come visit us. He'd eagerly pack his suitcase well ahead of his trip to Oz. He never spent money on himself, and so he'd recycle his holiday wardrobe each time, packing a 'papsak' (goon bag) filled with whiskey between his clothes and gifts of clothes, toys and South African chocolates and chewing gum for the girls.

'You needn't bring me anything, Dad,' I'd always warn, but he couldn't resist bringing me something – usually gym wear. We'd run many half-marathons together over the years and had bonded over our mutual enjoyment of exercise. He'd always get excited as he handed his gift over, repeating how great I'd look wearing them and which ones I should match together.

'Ah, thanks, Dad. I love them!' I'd say, and then place them with all the other brand-new leggings and sports tops he'd bought for me but weren't my style. I never told him, knowing he could have used the money for other necessities. To him, giving to me was more important than his own needs, and it gave him a chance to make me happy.

Dad thought Australia was the best country in the world. He would admire the beautiful produce in supermarkets, the cleanliness of the streets and efficiency of our systems. I believe he loved his visits because for one week, his problems vanished, and he could feel better about himself while he helped me.

Ever since we were kids, Dad had been a 'Mister Mom.' He cooked, cleaned, helped with homework and every year, covered towers of schoolbooks in brown paper and plastic. Whatever domestication I inherited was passed on from him. He loved pottering about; enjoyed parenting; and when he came to visit, he'd run my errands, help with parenting chores, fix things that had been broken for months, cook meals and play with the children. He'd pack the girls' school lunches, take them to school every morning so I could get to work earlier, and chat to their teachers and other parents. Everyone always remarked what a lovely man he was. He loved me and the girls dearly, and was so proud of our successes. He'd walk the streets of Rose Bay, enter every shop to browse and talk, telling everyone who would listen that he was visiting his daughter 'who was a doctor, a psychiatrist' (even though I'd tell him no-one cared). His greatest joy was being of service to my happiness.

But now, the curtain was falling on our week together. He was packed and ready to leave the following morning.

'I am so glad you are leaving! I can't wait for you to go!' I yelled at him. Our exchange of harsh words was a horrible closing act. Though it was our final night together, we spent it alone, each in our dark room, sadly silent.

The next morning, his suitcase stood at the front door, ready to be wheeled out. The taxi was on its way. We said our goodbyes. The girls sobbed. I told myself I was glad he was leaving, until the taxi pulled up in the driveway and then it felt as if sadness had pulled up and parked inside my heart.

We spoke few words. Our pain was too big, and it filled the space that would soon be a lonely, silent void. Dad looked at me, his eyes watery; but he tried to be brave, not wanting to upset me.

'Thank you so much for everything you do for me, for us. You are an amazing person,' he said.

I put my arms around him and held him tightly, knowing in the abstract way of many of our previous farewells that it could always be the last time.

'I'm sorry, Dad. I loved having you here. I'll miss you. We all will,' I sobbed.

I then watched as he wheeled his suitcase to the taxi, where he greeted the taxi driver with a handshake. Then he thanked the man for lifting the heavy suitcase and placing it in the boot. He looked back a final time and yelled out, 'Keep it up. You're doing great. Proud of you.'

He opened the rear door of the taxi, got in and closed the door. Then he rolled down the window as the taxi reversed and gave a gentle last wave.

'Bye, Dad! Travel safely! Love you!' I hope he heard my cries.

Then I went back into the house, which felt like a mortuary, silent and cold without him. His presence was everywhere even though he was no longer there. I walked down the long passage, peered into every room, visualising him playing, cleaning, putting on *Tefillin* in his underpants, reciting the morning Jewish prayer, the *Shema,* by heart as he'd done every day since his bar mitzvah, and in recent years, accompanied by pleas for God to give him a car sale.

The rooms were the same, only emptier.

In my room, I fell face down on my bed and wailed.

I could never have imagined that would be the last of Dad's very special visits to Australia.

* * *

When people claimed my father had taken his life, I did not believe it.

But without any proof or closure, not knowing what happened to him gnawed at my sanity. When life doesn't make sense, we grasp at anything that might provide a plausible explanation.

I'd just returned to Sydney from Dad's funeral and decided to see a psychic. Admittedly, this isn't my go-to for problem solving complex situations, but I'd consulted a highly recommended one years before, following confusing and hurtful relationship breakups. These were also times of desperation in my life – not comparable to Dad's death, of course – where I'd hoped for some reassurance that either the relationship would reignite in the future, or I'd find an alternate source of happiness again. The first time, I picked out the psychic's words that I wanted to believe were true, like dishing up only the more appetizing food on a smorgasbord. The second visit, she'd repeated the exact same lines she'd spoken the first time, so I never returned to her again.

But after Dad's death, I was prepared to give anything a chance once more; and one random day, without any proper research or recommendation, I entered a crystal store near my office. I'd seen them advertising the services of a psychic before, and I told myself that if there was an immediate appointment available, it was a sign. And there was.

I paid and entered a tiny dark room separated by a red velvet curtain from the retail section of the store.

I sat across from an ordinary-looking woman who casually asked what I wanted help with. Dubious of her credibility, I didn't want to give away any telepathic cues. She had to come up with the goods herself.

Anxiously, I replied, 'I want to know what happened to my dad. He died recently.'

I deliberately withheld facial expressions and verbal prompts so that I could trust her feedback.

Like a croupier, she was slick in shuffling a deck of tarot cards and told me to pick five. I ran my fingers over the smooth surface of the deck and silently asked Dad to guide my choice. I slowly pulled out five and handed them to her. She laid them down on the awkwardly low table between us.

Then she forewarned, 'If it's too soon, or the deceased doesn't really believe in the supernatural, they don't always present themselves to me.'

Dad would have been in the latter category of non-believers. He always dismissed anything he considered fluffy or airy-fairy – as he'd often done with my profession.

That day, I hoped he'd give her the benefit of the doubt and show himself to her, seeing as it was for my benefit.

She asked to see a photo of my father and explained it helped in tough cases.

Thanks, Dad, I thought. I passed her an image of Dad on my phone.

She examined it closely, then looked up at me and stated confidently, 'There was a fight…about money. There are three people. A man and a woman and your dad. He is standing next to a "ute." He is panicked. Trying to explain where the money is.'

Shocked and cold, I was unable to respond.

She continued, 'He is arching over, grabbing at his chest as if in pain. Was he shot? Or did he have a heart attack?'

I quickly replied, 'Neither.'

She went on to say that Dad was tired of scrambling. He was sorry for not letting us know of his struggles, but that now he was okay. I was completely freaked by the apparent truthfulness of all these statements. Her words leaned towards a murder, but she struggled to be conclusive. I wondered whether she didn't want to let me down; didn't really know; or was, in fact, reading my feelings and picked up on my doubts.

For months afterwards, I stewed over this encounter, indecisive about the usefulness and meaning of what she'd offered. I revisited the conversation, hoping to find that one hidden clue that could finally provide me with a concrete, decisive answer. But it never happened. Her words were a mixture of unnatural precision, perceived nonsensical statements and unfilled gaps.

Eventually, I decided to simply trust my own understanding. The psychic had said he'd repeatedly arched over in pain, and I chose to interpret the arching over as a message that Dad was heartbroken. He must have been terrified at the end of his life, but every stab to his heart symbolised his agony at our anguish at being left behind to deal with the aftermath. Dad would never have intentionally hurt or disappointed us.

Failing to find answers, I began to look for evidence of Dad's presence in the world around me. I wanted to believe that certain signs were proof of his spiritual existence. In psychiatry, such thoughts are sometimes evident in psychotic patients and can be considered a referential delusion, but I knew I was in touch with reality. Nevertheless, I was moved when Dad's birthdate appeared in random places; his Facebook profile remained my number one follower for years after his death; a photo of Dad and Daniella appeared as a memory on my phone the weekend of her bat mitzvah; or my predictive text when I typed the word *dad,* followed by a message to my sister on her first birthday after his death when she was so depressed and not wanting to celebrate.

Had he been reincarnated and returned as the new puppy that we bought shortly after his passing? I wondered. The puppy closely resembled the first dog I had as a child, a French poodle that Dad loved, and over time, had begun to look like with similar pitch-black pupils and dark, grey-speckled curly hair. I'd stare into the dog's eyes waiting for a sign.

All this was going on while my scientific mind kept insisting I was ridiculous to keep imagining symbolism in purely coincidental events. I read somewhere that without true belief, the deceased won't ever appear; so I'd try hard to convince myself that I really believed, but my doubts remained an annoying impediment.

I've only had one experience that has challenged my mystical cynicism, four months after his death. It was on Daniella's bat mitzvah, which Dad was excited about attending and remains one of the main reasons I still cannot believe he committed suicide. On the day, I felt an unusual sensation as if Dad was there with us. It was more than just a feeling; it was a physical weightiness, a closeness that was smothering and stifling. I wanted to push him off and say, 'Dad, please, you are too close. Give me space. Please!' But I'd have only been pushing air.

That feeling has never happened to me again.

I'd be thrilled if it were true that Dad was with me that day and every day, watching over me and even talking to other dead people about me as he'd always done when he was alive. But my rational brain always overpowers the esoteric. It is not unusual in times of grief to swing between extremes and paradoxes of thought and belief. It's all part of the grieving process as we test our hearts and souls.

I'm content that Dad lives within me. His voice in my head is quietly loud. He continues to exist in the way I live and conduct myself each day, much of which has been shaped by his guidance.

I recently rediscovered a copy of some scribbled notes written shortly before he died, though I was unsure whether he'd written them weeks, days or hours before his death. His final correspondence was not a loving letter, but a scrawled page in a diary of information he knew would be important to us. I was about to re-analyse it forensically, scouring it for anything I'd previously missed because I'd been in dire shock the first time I'd seen it.

But in that moment, I stopped myself and simply stared lovingly at his handwriting – it was such a familiar part of my life. Mum's handwriting is illegible, so she always asked Dad to write letters, cards and notes.

I ran my fingers over his shorthand, as I visualised him at his desk, rushing to do his best to leave us with these valuable details. It was endearing to sense that until his final moments, Dad wanted to ensure our wellbeing.

* * *

It is Yom Kippur, the day of Atonement, and the most holy day for Jewish people. I am more spiritual than religious, but I find myself in a synagogue. Somehow, I feel Dad's presence here. He always had faith in God, even though times were so tough for him. His beliefs seemed to get him through when he had nothing else to fall back on. When he needed answers, he turned to God. It gave him comfort.

I close my eyes and feel even closer to him. *Yizkor*, the memorial service for the dead, is recited on Yom Kippur, and literally means, 'May He (God) remember.' Only those who have lost a parent, child or sibling remain in the synagogue for this part of the service when Jewish people believe we are closest to our loved ones who have passed on.

In the past, I have always left before *Yizkor*, hardly looking at those still sitting in the pews. This time, I remain quietly in my seat. As I look around me, I realise every other person is hurting as much as I am as they remember their lost relative. I wonder how many of us have been left with unanswered questions or open loops that can never be sealed. Each one of us has our story of loss. It is a universal experience that connects us tangibly.

It is my first *Yizkor* as a bereaved child. As the service commences and the prayers are recited, I become teary.

'He will avenge the blood of His servants, bring retribution upon His enemies... I will cleanse...their wrongdoings, but for the shedding of...blood I will not cleanse them...'

I wonder if I will ever have answers, and if those responsible will ever pay for what they did. *I love you, Dad, and miss you so much.*

* * *

As the fast day draws to an end, the energy in the synagogue becomes electric, and the rising crescendo of beautiful melodies enhances the sense of elation and awe. My body tingles, and I feel an intense connection to something far bigger than myself. I am lightheaded from the lack of food and water, almost in a dissociative state. I recognise my nothingness in the world; yet at the same time, I feel real, raw and grounded within myself and the person I seek to be. As the final minutes draw near, I no longer feel the physical sensation of hunger.

The sound of the ram's horn, the *shofar*, thunders. It is

a symbolic call to attention, to be better, and to remember and honour Dad.

I will always miss my father. His death remains surreal. And although I see my growth, his loss still remains my greatest pain. I have no answers. I cannot get back what is lost. I cannot change what has happened; but I can continue to learn, refrain from judging, and deepen my understanding. In this way, I can keep growing. Part of that growth is in sharing my story with you in the hope that through it, you come to realise your worth and ability if you have ever doubted them.

It is in the far-reaching darkness of suffering that the slightest light illuminates the way out.

Acknowledgements

Words are wonderful. They have given me a way to express my thoughts, my feelings and my journey. They have provided the most wonderful memoir and honouring of my father.

I would not be here today without my father and his guiding light. Thank you, Dad. Thank you for bringing me into this world. Thank you for what you have given me and what you have not – it has all shaped me. Thank you for having good intentions. Thank you for allowing me to be myself and loving me. I will miss being close to you as I've felt whilst writing this book. I will grieve you eternally. I love you today, tomorrow and forever.

If ever I've come to love and respect another human being, it is my mother – the woman who gave me life. She has surpassed my expectations and my shame. Her strength through the darkest hours and the kindness she bestows upon me and all those around her are irreplaceable gifts. I cannot honour my mother sufficiently in words, but I can give thanks. I love you, Mommy, and I always will. Thank you for supporting me, loving me, tolerating me and teaching me what it means to survive against all the odds. You are forever my queen.

My children, Daniella and Rachel, I can say the words, 'I love you and you are my life,' but more importantly, I hope you feel those words deep in your hearts. I have been a busy mother and pushed you to fend for yourselves when perhaps all you have wanted is what I did – a more present mother. I acknowledge your hurt, offer my apologies and hope I have illuminated the paths of your potential. I believe in both of you. Thank you for understanding my hard work and giving me opportunities every day to be a better person.

To Simon, my partner. Your support is in the doing, not the words. I lean on you and you carry my weight, break my fall and lift me higher than I knew I could ever go. Thank you for everything and for listening to every chapter and story. Thank you for the solid advice. I love you.

Joanne Fedler, your kindness and generosity is the most admirable of human qualities. Your wisdom and your ability to use words is humbling. I can never thank you enough for your mentorship and guidance. Thank you so much. I have the utmost respect for your work ethic and humanity.

To every reader, thank you for choosing this book. I only hope it has provided you with a sense of your own possibilities that lie within each of you. For every trauma sufferer, person or family member afflicted with challenges to their mental health, I wish you healing and the courage needed to persist on this journey. You are my inspiration. I hope this book has given you a boost to continue to strive for better mental health. If anything between these pages helps just one person, I will be happy.

If you'd like to be in touch, you are welcome to share your story with me at mail@awarehub.com.au.

There is no quick fix to the struggles we face. Life is a series of hard and dark times. I hope this book offers a small light along your path. Because where there is light, there is hope.

Dr Lisa Myers
Sydney, May 2022

Printed in Australia
AUHW020738240922
369324AU00003B/3